Jose Silva
Research Scientist

# Silva Mind Control ®

## THROUGH

# PSYCHORIENTOLOGY

BY:

HARRY McKNIGHT

Dedication and Epilogue: Concepts
By:
Jose Silva

*10th Anniversary Edition*

REVISED, 1975, 1976.

# DEDICATION

This book is dedicated to:
The honorable creators of our galaxy, the Milky Way, that through these works we creatures will now evolve to our full potential.

Jose Silva

Copyright 1972, 1973, 1975, 1976 by Jose Silva. All rights reserved, including the right to reproduce this book, or portions thereof, in any form, except for the inclusion of brief quotations in a review. All inquiries should be addressed to Institute of Psychorientology, Inc., 1110 Cedar Avenue, Laredo, Texas 78040. This book was manufactured in the United States of America by the Institute of Psychorientology, Inc.

## Contents

Dedication — IV

Note — V

1. You are cordially invited to an opening seminar — page 1
2. The inside and outside of senses — 12
3. Definitions and analogies — 22
4. How you develop your Mind Control Method — 36
5. By your fruits you shall know — 50
6. Programming end-results — 60
7. The second phase of human evolution leads to the third — 72

Epilogue: Concepts by Jose Silva — 79

A select bibliography — 91

## NOTE

This special 10th/200th edition commemorates the 10th anniversary year of the Mind Control Basic Lecture Series being offered to the public and the 200th anniversary of the United States standing tall for freedom. It is fitting, then, that the Mind Control Series be now offered to the public as the American Dynamic Meditation System™.

Mind Control's Dynamic System brings a balanced approach to people helping themselves through meditation and programming. The ability that each of us has to imagine and visualize at a meditative level and use that information for problem solving is being researched more than ever by healing arts specialists in all professional walks of life, including the medical field. In controlling our subjective abilities, we do control our bodies and our minds. And the results are well-being, success, and abundance, all that is freedom's birthright. Graduates are also reporting improvements in business, education, and religion. In fact, Mind Control is practical for all participants, regardless of age. In addition, Mind Control has successfully been shared in all points of the globe with varied cultures and in many different languages.

Many graduates and students have asked for an introductory work that could be shared with friends concerning Silva Mind Control Method. They confessed that it was quite a challenge to sit with a friend over coffee or tea and discuss

## NOTE

the Silva Method adequately. They frequently commented that it takes a qualified lecturer the two or three hours of an opening lecture to share even basic ideas intelligently. In an attempt to meet that need the present brief work is offered.

You will find that this work is for you and about you. In the first chapter, you are asked to go through one person's experience of discovering the Silva Method so that you can discover your own experience. And even if you are already a graduate, you will enjoy reliving your own experience captured in this work. The remaining chapters help you to realize for yourself how you can help yourself and help others help themselves. Entering the Kingdom is the key; the message is working according to lawful relationships and allowing everything you need to come to you and yours.

This present work represents only the start of the first of many publications concerning the Silva Mind Control Method which is an outgrowth of Psychorientology, the new science. Since the first publication of this book, hundreds of thousands of graduates have been added to the swelling ranks of Mind Control people and many of them have authored articles and books directly or indirectly commenting upon the effectiveness of the Silva Method. Hopefully you will continue to help write them.

1

You are cordially invited to an opening lecture . . . .

Meeting Jose Silva was one of the most exciting series of moments in my life. There were about sixty of us gathered for an opening lecture on Mind Control Method. We had either been brought by friends or we had been attracted by an ad in the newspaper. Friends and the ad said that we were to hear about a breakthrough in the field of ESP research. The lecture was to be given by the man himself, a lay research scientist in the field of parapsychology. The man was Jose Silva.

The first man who greeted us after we took our places and waited some minutes beyond the scheduled time for the lecture was not Jose Silva. In fact, when the man began to introduce Jose and continued for about fifteen minutes, I almost got up and walked out. He spoke of having driven a nail through the palm of his hand while moving boards that day. He even held up his hand to show us the wound as he removed a strip of tape. His point: he had been able to remove the sense of pain and had stopped the bleeding--all by the Silva Method. He then went on to tell us, in somewhat uncultivated English, that we would be able to do more than that. I blanched. Caring for punctured hands was not my "bag." My field was counseling psychology and I was doing research during an internship, all part of the work for a Ph. D. in educational psychology.

It all began--my attending that opening lecture--when the supervisor of nurses on the ward where I was serving as a counselling psychologist under supervision said that there was a man I ought to meet. "Oh," I said, "who's that?"

"Oh, he's a man interested in the mind. He has a method for training people to use more of their mind."

"What's his name?" I inquired.

"Jose Silva," came her quick reply.

"Jose Silva!? Never heard of him," I retorted. And it was a retort, because I fancied that I was pretty up to date on things mental, since my field was psychology. After all, you don't spend hours in class, in discussion and in books and research and not come across significant people in your field.

"He's a lay researcher in parapsychology," she added, and I wondered if she was a bit smug in her reply.

I gave her the benefit of the doubt because she was really arousing my curiosity. I had come to respect her on the ward because of her positive attitudes of thought and health; you see, we were professional helpers on a rehabilitation ward and many of our patients were veterans from the Vietnam war--or whatever--and the way we thought about their well-being was important. In fact, my dissertation research was on attitudes of mind as related to successful discharge of patients from a rehabilitation ward. I saw that there was a positive correlation between a patient's attitude and his claiming health and rehabilitating himself. But I had not gathered data for statistical analysis to prove that fact - that's why I was in that particular hospital in that particular city at that particular time. At least, that's what I had thought my purpose was--but then, maybe I was there so I would meet Jose Silva.

"Parapsychology," I mused, half aloud.

"Yes," she said. "You would be interested in the work he is doing."

"Well, tell me about it," I said. "How does he teach you to use your mind?"

"I'm not quite finished with the courses yet," she replied. "And I really don't feel I can discuss it properly with you. Why don't you go hear him yourself? I'll bring you some literature that you can read."

"OK, I'd like to see it," I said.

It seems that my nurse guide was involved in some basic series and I had to wait until Mr. Silva ("Hmm, not Doctor," I thought. It was not until later that the Sangreal Foundation, represented by Carr P. Collins, Jr., awarded Jose Silva the honor of Doctor of Humanities for his outstanding accomplishments in the Mind Control program.) would be in town two months later before they were open for new enrollees. At the beginning of the basic series, he would have a free opening lecture so people could come to hear him and judge for themselves.

Time passed, but in the interim the nurse brought me literature about the course work and a book on Edgar Cayce. I had never really looked into parapsychology; I had heard it debunked in my classes on campus, and I knew literally nothing about Edgar Cayce--no, I take that back. My wife Alice had told me about a lecturer she had heard, sponsored by some way-out church group. The lecturer was Hugh Lynn Cayce. I especially remember because we had puzzled through that odd pronunciation of "case" to be "case-e." Well, anyway, I read the literature and devoured the book.

It really caught my attention and seemed to introduce me to all sorts of possibilities. I began to ponder the fact that Cayce was doing what the early Christian Church people had been able to do, not only the Apostles. He was having visions and dealing in prophecy and healing. And he was simply another human being. "That's interesting," I thought. "Maybe parapsychology has applied aspects I haven't heard of?" was the next enlightened question to cross my mind.

Would you believe that I was so filled with expectancy when I walked into that opening lecture that warm night in August 1968, that I felt almost like I was going to a new planet for the first time? I had shared all this with my wife and in telling her, I guess I built up even more curiosity. We used to sit around (Alice was expecting our second child) and exchange ideas about the kind of things that we had heard and read of that were related. We had read inquiringly into Christian Science, had poured through such volumes as Baird T. Spalding's Life and Teachings of the Masters of the Far East, The Urantia Book, and Human Destiny, just to mention a few of our metaphysical readings, but some of the most treasured ones. (Cf. A select bibliography.) She was almost as eager as I, but we decided that I be the guinea pig and go to the opening lecture before getting us involved. After all, we thought, it would be less embarrasing for one to walk out than two.

But I didn't walk out. I felt like I should stay and let Jose Silva speak for himself. If I walked out without hearing him, I would never truly know if I had made a wise decision. That kind of tenacity has served me in good stead, by the way. Many are the times I felt like abandoning a project but held on to see it unfold in exquisite fulfillment. As the little, round man went on about the glories of Mind Control Method, I sort of slouched in my chair with body language that shouted to anyone curious enough to notice me. But I tried not to distract the others. After all, if they wanted an evening of charlatan's fare, that was their business.

"Come on," I thought shoutingly in my mind, "bring on the man."

Maybe the little, round man heard me, because he began his peroration and pretty soon we were applauding another little man who was walking toward the podium. He was short, but of well-built stature, with greying, crew cut hair, and a nose. I remember the parrot-like nose. Maybe it wasn't the nose I noticed so much as the eyes. They seemed to be almost as black as his pupils, and it wasn't until later that I saw they were a deep brown. As he began to speak, I quickly adjusted to his Spanish overlay and mused at how forceful he could be in relatively flawless English. He spoke with authority and considerable erudition, though highly specialized. I was unable to decide if I detected a defensive quality in his tone or not. You see, I assessed and evaluated as any good therapist would.

As he progressed through what I later came to see was a well-prepared presentation, especially because it was based on personal experience that convinces, I felt a wedge opening my mind. It was as though a shaft of light penetrated my brain and unlocked areas that had lain dormant far too long--nay, had been repressed and denied. He spoke of subjective communication and solving problems and leaving this a better world to live in. He talked of research with youngsters who could not only get information clairvoyantly but could solve problems in many illustrative situations, not only health. I was amazed, to say the least. I hung on every word and waited for him to get to the part about our learning how to do all those things. Then came the refreshment break.

Since my nurse friend had told me that I would have an automatic scholarship because I was a psychologist, I felt the break would be a good time to sign up with the others for continuing coursework the next night. After all, an investment of time was all I was making, and he had already proven to be an engaging lecturer, if only for his content. When I took the completed registration card to the two ladies who were enrolling students, my nurse friend (she was one of the ladies enrolling and who sponsored Jose Silva's going to that city) suggested that I have Mr. Silva initial my card as an approval on the scholarship arrangement.

Waiting to see Mr. Silva was like queueing up for autographs after a sell-out theatre performance. He was literally being overwhelmed with enthusiastic questions from eager members of the audience. Finally he noticed me.

"Mr. Silva," I said, "the lady suggested I get your approval for a scholarship. I'm not a psychologist yet, but I am finishing up my dissertation research now." I handed him the card confidently.

"Oh," he said. "There must have been a mistake. There is a scholarship for psychologists who are heads of departments." He smiled, trying to reassure me; then someone quickly got his attention with another question.

I was crestfallen, I guess. I returned to the registration desk and told her the outcome. She apologized and suggested that I not give up but approach him again later in the evening. My spirits lifted slightly.

Needless to say, after the next portion of lecturing, I was more enthusiastic than before. And impatient to get on with the course work! Come the break, I approached Mr. Silva and made sure to get him off to privacy on the side. He cooperated humbly.

"Mr. Silva," I said, "I think you have the most exciting ideas I have heard in a long time. I feel like I want to instruct and do research with you, if I go through the courses successfully, and they <u>are</u> what you say. But I feel I cannot afford to put out money for the course right now. I am on a limited stipend, my wife is expecting, and I don't feel I should take our savings for your courses at this time."

In a flash, with no interim for puzzling, Mr. Silva replied. There I was, all prepared to present more briefing of my case, and he stopped me with a simple, straightforward reply.

"O K," he said. "Give me your card."

With that, I handed him the card; he initialed it and hardly waited to hear my "Thank you." He walked back to where students eagerly awaited him, and I hurried to the desk with the good news. That was the beginning of what has since become a firm and lasting friendship and business association. I did go on to do research and instruct with Jose Silva, because I finished the courses successfully and they were _more_ than he had said. In fact, I'm still uncovering their depth of meaning for humanity.

When I returned home that night, I shared as much as my wife's sleepy ears would attend to. We quickly determined that I would share all with her as I progressed. She could later take the work as she wanted and felt able to. As it turned out, she started the work in October and we both successfully completed the work in the first graduating class in Houston that December, 1968. And Alice expecting all the while!

As I bubbled with enthusiasm, Alice gathered in the facts of that first evening. I related how Mr. Silva, way back in 1944, began his inquiries into mind and its functioning. He had been inducted into the Signal Corps and when the Army examiners passed him on to the examining physicians, one examiner piqued his curiosity by asking psychiatric type inquiries that seem sometimes idiotic to the healthy mind. Jose related how he figured that the man must know a lot about the mind and that he was evidently asking the questions for a purpose, so he engaged him in as much conversation as time then would permit.

So began Jose's odyssey. He subsequently turned his attention more and more from his specialty of electronics and devoted reading time to Freud, Jung, Adler, and other giants in the field of analysis. As he studied more deeply, he realized that psychology, particularly as it began to focus in the States about that time (late 40's into the 50's,) was turning its research attention away from the mind as such and was investigating and theorizing about observable behavior that could be physically measured and mathematically expressed. That meant Jose had to look elsewhere for further inquiry into the nature and workings of the human mind. He delved into metaphysical works and eventually versed himself in things parapsychological. Alongside all this reading and study, Jose's practical bent brought him to the decision that he should experiment for himself and test out some of the hypnotheses he was reading about. Could he replicate some of the research himself?

It was then that Jose steeped himself in all literature available to him in the field of hypnotic research. He sensed that Freud had erred in abandoning such research. (Unfortunately Freud was not an excellent hypnotic technician and the nature of the patient population he sampled limited him even more.) The whole field of hypnoanalysis may have been flourishing much sooner had Freud first studied with Liebeault and Bernheim rather than Charcot. Jose developed expertise as a hypnotic researcher, though lay, and by beginning with his own children, started helping youngsters improve their Grade Point Average and I.Q. factor. He got quite a reputation in Laredo, Texas, and was well-known as a lecturer and researcher in regression in his home town. It was in the early 50's that he had come upon the startling discovery that the subjects in his research could answer questions he had not yet asked! When he redesigned his research and focused on the so-called "Guessing phenomenon," he discovered that the youthful subjects could get information other than through their so-called five senses.

By 1949 he personally had accomplished enough self-development that he could systematize his use of subjective levels of mind, or that dimension of information processing other than the five-senses dimension. Come 1953 he had proven that he could train a subject to develop these latent abilities to get information at subjective levels and to use that information to solve problems. He had achieved the repeatable experiment in investigating the psi factor. His subject could accomplish what Dr. John Elliotson had demonstrated in his two subjects who diagnosed clairvoyantly, as Elliotson reported in his "Harveian Oration" in 1846. Correspondence with Dr. J. B. Rhine, then at Duke, proved fruitless, so Jose determined to continue on his own, convinced that he could use his method to help others uncover, develop, and apply their similar abilities for problem solving.

After more years of research, both public and private, none of which was ever recorded for publication so that posterity could admire, Jose worked with individuals and groups. Word about his researched methods got out in 1966 to the public beyond Laredo. Dr. N. E. West, then psychologist at Wayland Baptist College in Plainview, Texas, invited Jose to lecture to his students. Other than Dr. J. Wilfrid Hahn, physical chemist and now Chief Scientist for Silva Mind Control International, Inc., who was Jose's closest and most encouraging consultant, Jose had few supporters in the academic world who would step forward to support and encourage him. He always paid his own way through it all, however, and is able to say that Mind Control Method not only supported itself but also now supports others who are doing research in the Silva Method.

As word travels, it reached the ears of Dord Fitz, artist, instructor and entrepreneur of art in Amarillo, Texas. He had been functioning for years as a natural psychic but did not know how to teach others to uncover and use that ability in themselves. When he heard that this man in Laredo had perfected a teaching method, he invited Jose to address his art students. That October, 1966, marks the first time Jose started Mind Control Classes in English. The incident had its humor.

The students who had been gathered from all over the Panhandle of Texas and Oklahoma were so excited once they heard about Jose Silva's research that they begged him to teach them Mind Control Method. He said that he had never taught classes in English before. They quickly countered with, "That's all right. You teach us Mind Control Method and we'll teach you English!" To this day, graduates of that first English Mind Control class are functioning and supporting the work in their individual ways. Some have even gone on to become lecturers themselves! And the movement continues to spread.

In 1966 formal classes were started in Mexico, and they are presently under the National direction of Juan Silva, Jose's brother who is a Mind Control-developed inventor. From 1966 to February 1969, Jose was the only one offering the Silva Method in the United States. And it was that warm evening in August, 1968 that brought him his first lecturer to join him full time in the States. But it wasn't until February of 1969 that he was able to share the task with the author.

And that brings us back to Alice's sleepy ears. When I realized that much of what I had been saying had fallen on her pillow for the night, I retired with far more of an open mind than I had taken to that opening lecture. Recounting some of that exciting evening to my wife had made me realize an observation attributed to Napoleon. He was often the butt of jokes about his short stature. On some occasion or other he is reported to have said, "The height of a man is not measured from his head to the ground, but from his head to the sky!" I've since heard Jose Silva jokingly use that quotation as a semi-retort in similar situations. That night, as I drifted off to sleep, I couldn't help but marvel at what that man had brought to light on this planet of ours. He quietly refers to it as the beginning of the second phase of human evolution. My heart leaped at the thought that I was becoming part of it.

2

## The inside and outside of senses

When prospective participants enter opening Mind Control lectures, or seminars, however they are designated, one of the first items to catch their attention is the chart depicting the Scale of Brain Evolution. (Cf. Chart page 93, copyrighted by Jose Silva.) Before he has gotten too far into the material the lecturer explains the chart to the prospective Mind Control graduates. He will usually comment on current brain research that is before the public's eyes, because he knows that they have come to hear about a subject that is somewhat unknown to them and he would do well to make a transition from the known to the unknown. He will typically incorporate the latest findings, always tentative, that scientists knowledgeable in the field of brain wave research have published. In this way, he talks about the next best thing that physical scientists have uncovered with relation to the mind: the brain and its rhythms and functioning.

As the lecturer knows, one of the most difficult parameters or variables or factors to measure is mind. Particularly do behavioral scientists agonize in that regard because they have limited themselves by and large to items that are amenable to physical measurement: observable behavior; <u>observable</u> to the five senses, that is. (In the next chapter we will understand that there are other senses, called inner senses, different from the five senses.) After all, a research scientist can observe interpersonal relationships in a group, can get outside judges to agree or not within statistically confident limits about observable behavior, and can measure changes in health status detectable as physiological or reputed psychological effects of some treatment process. But how can one measure the mind by those standards? How long is the mind when you place it next to a ruler? What color is it? Because of these physical measurement criteria, parapsychological research has been stagnated at academic levels of inquiry. It took a lay researcher from Laredo to break the lock-step error. Jose Silva realized that to measure the mind one needs a much sharper instrument than physical science had yet produced. He realized that he had to use the basis of all tool-making, the reflective awareness of man, called mind. After all, he reasoned, isn't that what the scientists are using to interpret their criterial measures? One needs to use mind to measure mind. Mind is the only adequate instrument of measuring itself. But that sounded so circular that scientists have for years looked down on introspection. As a result, they seemed to think that mind-type phenomena were irrelevant to scientific investigation in the behavorial sciences and inapplicable with regard to scientific method.

The tide is changing ebb and flow, however, as current revival of humanism in psychology witnesses. Of similar testimony is the spate of sensitivity-type approaches to psychotherapeutics, and the varied biofeedback training approaches in medical therapeutics, particularly as regards psychosomatic illnesses. Of significance also is the well-established research, both theoretical and applied, in the field of the various behavior therapies. All these aspects of the health-caretaking Zeitgeist witness to a true phase of evolution being enacted in this our seventh decade before the year of 2000. That research scientists in the various disciplines are coming to understand man as a functioning organism in an environment lends hope to the future. They are using advances in technology, especially the field of electronics, to mirror man himself in his reflected creations. His toy and tool making enables him to look upon himself with greater perceptive awareness, describe himself and understand himself more than he ever has in our recorded history. And if physically he cannot yet measure mind, he is doing the next best thing. He is measuring brain waves, brain activity, and he is beginning to make headway in studying obvious and not-so-obvious physiological and psychological correlates. To measure the brain is not to measure the mind, because they are not the same thing, as we will come to understand. But to measure brain is to measure the seat or organ of mind functioning par excellence.

The Scale of Brain Evolution (see page 93) is sort of a descriptive map of the relationship between brain and mind. It is this chart that every Mind Control Lecturer shares with the new students at opening lectures. The lecturer explains that it reflects the best in research to date in the field, though the findings are tentative. After all, the scientific method is self-correcting; as more data come in, the previous findings have to be interpreted in the light of new facts uncovered. Although given considerable creative scope, the lecturer starts usually by pointing out that the brain operates on about 25 watts of electrical power and that the brain's electrical activity causes a voltage to appear through the skull and scalp which can be detected by EEG (Electroencephalograph) types of equipment. The basic units of measurement to describe this energy are the microvolt and cycles per second (CPS). A cycle (as in bi<u>cycle</u>) means a circle or completed revolution from beginning to end. The cycle in current which is AC can be expressed in amplitude (height), polarity (+ or -) and frequency. (Cycle: A complete set of recurrent values as one complete positive alternation and one complete negative alternation of an alternating current. Usually represented by the sine curve.) DC pulsating cycles appear like AC current, although it is DC in itself. (Pulsatory Current: continuous current, constant in direction, but periodically varying in intensity so as to progress in a series of throbbings or pulsations, instead of with uniform strength.) That you can have certain frequencies per second gives the term "cycles per second," or CPS. If we start at the lower hash mark of the chart, we notice at the bottom that we have Delta, flanked by a question mark and the word "Unconscious." The hash marks in this band of frequencies go up to about 4 CPS from approximately .5 CPS. That band of frequencies is about the lowest detectable by present day equipment. Naturally, 0 CPS would mean, if it continues, a brain that is not functioning. But in a live brain scientists typically uncover some EEG activity.

The question mark indicates that scientists simply have few researched facts in the laboratory published to know what is going on there. We rarely have self-reported awareness to indicate a level of consciousness so we call it "Unconsciousness." There is awareness there, as we shall see in the last chapter, and we may be able to control it some day, as we think the most developed adepts in our planet's history have. To date, however, scientific findings concerning Delta awareness are limited.

As we move up the scale of hash marks, we reach the 4-7 CPS band of frequencies. This is referred to as the Theta range of brain waves. The Theta frequencies are now being researched as the most significant frequencies in certain problem solving by animals and man. They are typically correlated with levels of sensitivity to pain, etc. Deep regression studies and reincarnation-type studies can be done when the subject is functioning in a controlled way at Theta frequencies. Professionals involved in psycho-therapeutics using altered states of consciousness find this range most effective for many deep-seated problems and for reconditioning behavioral patterns.

The next range of frequencies, the Alpha rhythms, from about 7 - 14 CPS on our chart, is of particular interest. Although both Alpha and Theta are Inner Conscious dimensions, we are establishing controls particularly of the Alpha, with control of the Theta following upon more training and practice for problem solving, as we will discuss more at length in Chapters 6 and 7. It was the Alpha rhythm that Berger first discovered in the late 20's. For a time these Alpha rhythms were referred to as Berger rhythms, but later were renamed according to the present terminology. These frequencies are sometimes called "R E M Area" depending on what frequencies you accept as Alpha, 8 – 12 or 7–14) because in dream and sleep research, it has been found that the eyes can rapidly move when a person is dreaming; thus, Rapid Eye Movement, abbreviated R E M. Further research indicates that there is also <u>Non-REM</u> dreaming, however, so we present that bit of information tentatively about Alpha. If you want an indication of Alpha production, you can close your eyelids, turn your eyes slightly upward, and your eyelids start to flutter. This flutter accompanies a stronger Alpha output on the Alpha

Sensor, or similar types of feedback instruments so available on the present market.

Naturally, there is much more to discuss about the Alpha range and the Inner Consciousness positively correlated to it, but let us move on for now and return to the discussion later. That later discussion is what focuses the opening lecture evening, really.

As we examine the chart, continuing up the hash marks, we arrive at what are called Beta frequencies and Outer Conscious Levels. Beta is the less synchronized as far as energy is concerned but is the highest peaking in terms of brain wave frequencies. Beta ranges from about 14 to 21 CPS typically, but can spike up to 50 or 60 CPS, and even higher. As you read this book, look around at your surroundings, or listen to audible noises, you are functioning predominantly at Beta. You may have also a mixture of some Alpha and Theta; rarely do we seem to have a resting frequency or an unmixed frequency without training. Beta is the frequency of brain positively correlated with using your so-called five senses. It is the world that the physical sciences are detecting and measuring to uncover lawful relationships. It is the typical world of Time and Space categories known to philosophy and science. It has been estimated that adults without disciplining their minds function at Beta about 80% of the time. The other 20% are indicative of Alpha-Theta-Delta functioning, particularly at night when they sleep.

You see, nature has laid some rules down for our playing the game of life effectively. She says, as it were, that we must get Alpha-Theta and Delta-type frequencies, especially when we sleep at night, or we don't remain very healthy. In fact, our brain wave patterns typically fluctuate in and out of the various frequencies rather constantly during the waking day. People who have trained themselves seem to be exceptions to those rules, but only because they have learned how to proportion their frequency variations healthily and under their own control. Some people can do with less sleep at night because they have mastered a balanced variation in brain frequency alteration.

But what can we say about the Inner Conscious Levels of mind and the Alpha-Theta frequencies of brain? Since we will discuss Theta more at length later, let us concentrate on Alpha. Scientists in brain wave research have uncovered some interesting findings. We will discuss the brain activity and its attendant mind functioning.

One of the very significant findings to come out of brain wave research, particularly as conducted in sleep and dream research laboratories, is that when a person dreams at night, he is typically functioning at Alpha. At least, if you train a subject to tell you by verbal report what he is experiencing, and you waken him when he manifests R E M, he will tell you that he was dreaming, if you ask him what he was experiencing. That does not mean that there is no dreaming at Theta and/or Delta—it simply means that he can remember dreams if awakened from Alpha. And the research also shows that dream deprivation can be damaging mentally, emotionally, and physically. If we do not dream we do not stay healthy very long.

Another finding of note is that healing is significantly related to Alpha functioning. It is as though intelligence can manage energy more effectively if the brain is functioning at Alpha, and the 10.5 CPS frequency, more specifically. Once energy is under intelligent management, illnesses seem to vanish and healing can be much more effective. That is why physicians tell their patients to get bed rest after major surgery. When they are resting, the brain can dip into Alpha, so to speak, and the body can heal so much more effectively. Keep the brain busy at Beta and healing is slowed, maybe interrupted if the Beta activity is too violent. That is why biofeedback training is such a therapeutic novelty in medicine these days. The so-called autonomic functions can even be controlled through control of brain wave frequencies. Psychosomatic illnesses such as asthma, heart conditions, and migraine headaches vanish also, with time and practice.

We mentioned that the 10.5 CPS frequency was a desirable frequency. Why did we specify? Because when Berger rhythms were first discovered at about 10 CPS, we think his primitive detection devices must have picked up the most energetic frequencies. As detection devices became more sensitive, other frequencies could be described. The fact that the 10 CPS frequency is near the center of 0 to 21 CPS, we choose to refer to 10.5 CPS as being the center of the three octaves: Delta-Theta = .5 to 7 CPS, Alpha = 7 to 14 CPS and typical Beta = 14 to 21 CPS. Thus, the most synchronized energy is found at the center. Centering for synchronized energy seems to be of long-standing realiability. For example, the hub of the wheel is the strongest focus for synchronized energy. Horace, in another vein, said, "In media stat virtus," and freely translated that can mean "Energize by centralizing." It is as though we are tuned into all the healing forces in the universe of energy when we are centralized in our own brain frequency. And when we do it consciously, we have intelligent management as human beings should. After all, we are more human to the degree that we are more aware. And as we shall come to see, we are more loving to the degree that we are more aware. And that's what it's all about. To be human means to participate in loving (human) acts.

A third benefit from functioning at Alpha, especially under your own, natural control, is that the human mind becomes creative at these dimensions; and if we do not create, we go backwards personally and as a culture. The inventor, the artist, the healing specialists, the creative parent--all of us dip into Alpha more frequently when we are turned on. There seems to be a positive correlation between creativity and personal healing. That is why the creative mind seems not to age, although the body does; but a body guided by a creative mind ages less than usual, all things else being held constant. That is why artists, enthused with their present creative urge that they are expressing, can go for days sometimes without food and sleep that they ordinarily use when not creatively expressing. That is why creative health caretakers can labor with loving dedication in a plague-ridden area and rarely come down with the disease. Their creative functioning seems automatically to get them to the healing dimension where they are preserved from disease. But because endurance can be limited by poor discipline and improper intake of needed chemistry, there can be an eventual breakdown. But how long it can be averted!

Another benefit from Alpha functioning is that problem solving abilities are enhanced through programming. Particularly is this so when one actively controls entering, exiting, and time spent at Alpha. But we shall discuss this phase more at length in Chapter 6.

A final, but by no means the least, discovery to come from investigation of Alpha functioning is what Jose Silva discovered with children as subjects in his research. Here it is that so-called psychic functioning is enhanced. Here it is that it can be discovered, developed, and applied to solve problems. It is at Alpha Levels that people can train themselves to tap information not available through the five senses. A whole new dimension of information processing opens up to everyone versed in the Silva Method. It is so vast an area of resourcefulness that opens up to the graduate, and it takes no longer than 40 to 48 hours (youngsters can do it in half the time), that we liken it to the Christian message about the Kingdom. (Cf. <u>Matthew</u>, particularly Chapter 6.) If you seek your kingdom within, and function according to the laws you discover there, everything you need comes to you. It is the age-old counsel re-expressed but this time by one who could teach others how to do it validly and reliably. Buddha invited devotees to enlightenment. Socrates said, "Know thyself." But Jesus Christ had a message how to do it — Become like a child! So students in Mind Control Method become as childlike as quickly as possible.

Isn't it at least interesting that Jose Silva discovered the science and developed the method as he researched with children? They were the best subjects because they are the least biased, they tell things as they see them, and they have fertile imaginations. Imaginations--that's a key, isn't it? If we take a common denominator of characteristics at Alpha that are beneficial, we come up with dreaming, creativity, and psychic functioning as having imagination in common. Could it be that imagination is so unlocked at Alpha that Mind can use it for communication purposes that far exceeded what we thought typical and what is available at Beta? But what is mind, and how is it related to brain? Perhaps we should turn our attention to answering those and other questions before we continue on our journey of exploring an opening lecture in the Mind Control Method.

3

Definitions and analogies

In Chapter 2 we discussed the benefits of functioning in Alpha Levels. We saw that there are desirable effects in being able to 1) dream, 2) heal more effectively, 3) create, 4) program, and 5) communicate subjectively. We discussed some of these benefits but deferred others for later chapters. Let us discuss the relative merits of ways to alter levels of consciousness so that we can claim benefits at various ranges of frequencies. Then we will discuss mind and its relationship to brain.

There are three fundamental types of approaches to altering conscious states. We quite frankly think that some approaches are more advantageous than others. Two types are physically coercive and one is natural. By physically coercive we mean that some sort of outside agency is used to force electro-chemical changes in brain. Electronic stimulation and drugs are of this type. By natural we mean that the person alters his brain chemistry through variation in thought processes that are self-controlled and not precipitated by alien electronic stimulation or drug additives. Electronic and drug stimulants (and/or depressants) place the person's brain activity and related function in an outside dependency of control. The person is at most controlling his own function through an intervening agent rather than through his own information processing as such.

We have implied our persuasion already, haven't we? We can understand that it is far more beneficial for a person to control rather than to be controlled by outside forces. The rationale of science is to discover lawful relationships so that one can apply laws wisely for one's own development and that of all creation. Whenever we can do something for ourselves but we deliberately slough off our responsibility so that others must do it for us, we know we make a mistake. If everybody becomes the "taken-care-of" rather than the caretakers we would have a childish society and eventually would fall to the lowest of kingdoms in this world. So, if we can alter our brain frequencies by natural, Mind Control methods but choose to go the route of dependency on electronics or drugs, we are definitely limiting ourselves needlessly. Huxley's Brave New World and Orwell's 1984 have already foreshadowed technologically and drug-addicted man who needs others to do his thinking for him. The pictures sketched were not appealing. We create less than human when we abuse our controls.

To surrender controls needlessly is ill enough, but when surrendering controls is also physically and psychologically damaging to the organism, we have an act of insanity in such surrender. It is not denied that much investigative research is uncovering applications for electronic stimulation, but it is apparent injustice to people that other, less damaging means do not get at least equal time and funding. It is quite possible to create a robot-like person by controlling human behavior through electrode implantation, but is it desirable? It is quite possible to use electroshock therapy to "treat" certain psychiatric disorders, but is it desirable if there are other alternatives? If there can be mapping of the brain without physically insulting the skull and brain cells, what defense is there for mapping by electronic stimulation of a brain in a sawed-off skull?

Drug additives can be equally damaging if not more so. One of the severest and most harmful side effects is sludging of blood vessels. The brain cells consume vital chemicals that are conveyed by blood to the needy areas. If the blood vessels are not able to provide passage for necessary chemicals, the cells begin to die. The sad part is that to date, we do not know how to regenerate dead brain cells. We can sometimes re-educate other areas of the brain to do the job that needs to be done, but we have only about 14 billion brain cells to work with. Killing them needlessly is not the answer, whether by electronic stimulation or by chemicals. If you want to see the effects of killing brain cells, visit a hospital where there are returning soldiers from war-torn areas, or an alcoholic ward in the psychiatric sections of your local hospitals.

With the natural approaches to brain wave control you need not fear physical damage to your brain. Not only are you controlling but you are always guided by your survival programming to help, not hurt yourself. You process the information naturally and changes in brain chemistry follow automatically. You use your awareness to govern your brain activity, and you educate yourself so that you know how to do it wisely. Instead of creating problems, you solve problems. And that is what Silva Mind Control Method is all about. It is you using your human intelligence to alter brain frequencies naturally. It is the natural control of altered states of consciousness to solve problems. You see, there are states of mind that can be related to various ranges of frequencies. Changes in those frequencies can be brought about by altering your level of consciousness. It is mental control of brain rather than physical control of mind. It is poles apart from what Jose Delgado and others are doing with electronic implantation in brain whereby body functioning and behavior of all sorts can be controlled with the press of a button.

But what do we mean by mind? We promised ourselves a discussion. Well, let us perform a little experiment together that will help us arrive at a working definition and then let us use an analogy to clarify mind even further. After we have discussed those topics, we will then examine inner senses, psychic functioning and subjective communication.

As you read now you can concentrate on the book itself; you can interrupt your reading and attend to the quality of the paper and its texture. You can also divert your thoughts even more and look around you. You can listen for sounds in the environment. You can think about your clothes and how they feel. You can actually be aware, then, of your immediate experience. You can focus on it, attend to it, think about it. You are using what we call the mind. Your ability to reflect on your experience and be aware is your mind function. Your intelligence can also process the information that your mind is sensing. You can reason about the bits of information, analyzing and synthesizing into related bits, or you can simply admire and enjoy, or you can make value judgments, and so forth. You can work with the experienced information that you are aware of or that you are <u>mindful</u> of.

Not only can you focus on immediate experience, but you can also think back on or recall what you had to eat and drink at your last meal. Pick out your favorite dish from the menu you had. You can recall the taste, hotness or coldness, etc. You can recreate that experience of eating and drinking. You are using your mind to sense that recreated experience that has been stored in your information processing equipment, possibly your brain. Or you can think back on the most enjoyable day you had last year. Recall the people and the events. Recreate the situation. You think about it, you know it, you remember it, you imagine it, or daydream it—whatever you think you are doing, you are using your mind. You see, we all have one and we use it. In fact, those who deny that we can research the mind in a scientifically valid and reliable way are really denying that we can make the functioning of mind so operational that we can detect it, measure it, and make predictions from the data we uncover. They say that what we just did in attending to our experience, immediate and past, is not open for public verification. It is all private and introspective, they say. But they are incorrect. We will come to see in Chapter 4 that we can devise methods of scientifically demonstrating the reality of inner sensing and imagination—both mind functions. The mind is real and is open to detection and measurement by other minds.

What we have just done in our little exercises is to arrive at an operational definition of mind. Operational means that it is workable for our purposes. Let us describe mind verbally now. Mind is awareness, reflection, or focus of attention. It is thinking, imagining, perceiving. Mind is best described by its function, by a processing of information. When we process information which comes to us through brain functioning at Beta (the brain is using the five senses), we speak of our using our mind at an Outer Conscious Level (Cf. Chart page 93). As we attend to information coming to us through the brain functioning at Alpha and/or Theta frequencies, we are using our Inner Conscious Levels of awareness. Our mind is tuned in to inner sensing, not outer five-senses sensing. If we are deep in sleep, we are processing information through brain's functioning at Delta frequencies predominantly, and that we will discuss in Chapter 7. For now let us continue to call such processing an unconscious dimension or unawareness.

Our analogy will best serve us at this point. Imagine a submarine. Recall some of its characteristic features. It is usually a vehicle for carrying men; it has such adaptability that it can travel in or on water. It has a periscope that can be elevated above water for gathering information into its information processing center, when it is partially submerged. It also has sonar equipment for gathering information below the water's surface, in case it must navigate while completely submerged. The personnel in the submarine simply tune into their environment by periscope or sonar, or both alternately, if they need information to solve problems, such as in navigating a course, etc. The instruments allow for versatility. Now for our analogy.

The brain is similar to the submarine. The brain has senses that can pick up information from the environment. It can use its eyes, ears, nose, tongue and fingers to get information from the outside, surface environment the way the periscope picks up surface information for the submarine. Or it can use its sonar type equipment for picking up information only available at deeper levels under the surface. All the person on the submarine has to do is focus attention on the sonar scope. Intelligence is like the person seeking information. Intelligence may use the periscopic 5-senses if the desired information is above the surface or it may use the sonar-type equipment to search out bits of information and pattern within the deep. Intelligence simply tunes its sensing mechanisms to the proper channels and gets the information it needs to solve the particular problem at hand. The mind is the sensor of the intelligence. It is to the intelligence as the periscope and sonar equipment are to the submarine.

When intelligence needs information, it simply senses it through mind. Mind scans the layers of brain cells (Beta, Alpha, Theta, or Delta), so to speak, and senses on brain cell impressions the information intelligence is seeking, as your eye scans this page for words.

It was obvious from Jose Silva's research with youngsters and adults that one's ability to process information is vaster than the ability we display when we process information obtained through the five senses only. That is similar to the submarine being dependent only on information gotten by periscope. There is also sonar. You remember that the fifth benefit of functioning at Alpha Levels that we discussed in Chapter 2 was psychic functioning or subjective communication. Now we know what that is all about. It is all about our sonar, so to speak.

You see, the human is many-faceted, and can be looked at in many ways. We have been described as a rational animal, Homo sapiens (et amans, because Homo is also loving), a religious being capable of the I-Thou relationship, a social being, a political being, a person, a father, mother, son, daughter, an employer or employee, a biological entity studied in the life sciences, a humanitarian, a professional, a lay person, an artist, scientist, a teacher, student — the list could go on indefinitely, simply because the human, in general and in particular, is multi-dimensional. Humans can be defined differently accordingly as we are limiting ourselves to one point of view or another. Human is defined one way by chemistry, another way by biology, differently by philosophy, variously by psychology, another way by theology, and so forth. Different arts and sciences, both theoretical and applied, consider human from other specific viewpoints, accordingly as the particular art or science might demand. The formal boundaries of these varied contents, methods, and systematic bodies which make up arts and sciences determine what is or is not to be considered as material for study by an art of science.

More and more, however, the arts and sciences are linking arms, so to speak, in what is called an interdisciplinary approach to studying and helping humanity. Even the environment is being recognized as a powerful influence, as the spate of ecological studies especially since the '50's has shown. In other words, the human is coming to be studied, assessed, and evaluated as a dynamic agent of interaction in an environment; a person is looked at as a being capable of <u>becoming</u> through commerce with culture and sub-cultures. More and more we are looked upon as a vital awareness expressing itself in the experiential dimensions which are the life styles on this planet. We are a dynamic synthesis of all our experiences — and we are more: we are consciousness expressing a certain way through those experiences. We <u>are</u> and we <u>are</u> <u>becoming</u>.

Another way of putting it is to say that the human is in process. If one were to look at the gestating seed and ovum, become an egg in the womb of the mother, and were to allow one's self only that one glance as a basis for a prediction of what was developing, how inadequate would be the forthcoming statement about a person. How slight the statement about humanity's potential for speech would be, for example, if the only evidence for prediction were the one-month-old baby's sounds.

We are a totality in process and our experience helps to make us what we are. At any one point in the process we might seem extremely limited; add all the observations together and we stand tall as a synthesis of potentials and actuals, of possibles becoming realities. We are able to become what we are called to be. The stuff of life seems to be to help us fulfill ourselves rather than block our development. In other words, we have abilities to be what we can be and want to be. With proper guidance and a supportive environment we can achieve our destiny and be fulfilled.

While we are achieving our fulfillment we manifest various abilities. For example, as we sit at the piano and play the masters, we speak of our musical ability. Our paintings reflect our artistic ability in another creative dimension. When we theorize relativity and express the abstractions symbolically, we call it ability for mathematics and physics. When we express thanksgiving in a worshipful attitude of spirit, we speak of our ability for encounter, which is religion. As we run down the field for the winning touchdown or accept the trophy for outstanding Ping Pong, we speak of our athletic ability. But through it all, we are humanity revealing varied abilities. As our instruments become sharper and our criteria of measurement become more sensitive, we are able to measure more and more of the abilities which we reveal in our experiences.

Still another way of attempting to describe humanity is to examine people in all their functional relationships. How we function oftentimes reveals what we are able to do. As we function at home, at work, in school, privately, etc., we display many abilities to interact with our environment. Through this interaction we are both changed and changing. We assimilate influences from our environment and we accommodate to the needed changes brought about by such assimilation. In addition, we cause changes to come about in people and things around us. For example, if Mary comes up to you and angrily slaps your face, you have assimilated negative energy from your environment (presumably unwillingly and somewhat uncomfortably). How you respond to the situation will describe "accommodation." If you react by blindly slapping her face, you return negative energy to her; if you help her calm herself and turn off the negativity, you have responded quite differently. Both approaches to the situation would be types of accommodation, however.

Life can be described as a process of such assimilation and accommodation. Accordingly as people function in interactive situations, they can be said to reveal abilities of one sort or another. This is the foundation for considering that humanity has abilities of any kind. The ability is posited as a source for the functional action. If Mary slapped you, she obviously had ability to slap you. But consider an area of human ability that is not such a slap in the face. Consider intellectual ability. What is it?

Intellectual ability has been defined as that which is measured by I. Q. tests. That definition is rather circular, we think. We can do better than that, although that definition might serve well in a particular situation or operation. Intellectual ability really is our ability to interact with our cultural situation. Ability, as we have seen, is power to function; therefore, intellectual ability can be adequately defined as power to function in interactive relationships with cultural situations. Thus I. Q. is an index of measurement; it is a statement of a person's measured ability to interact with the environment in a functional relationship. It is a statement of our capability to conduct commerce with our environment. It can also be used as a factor helpful in predicting what the person will achieve in future commerce with that environment.

As you can determine, there are many abilities hidden in the term "intellectual ability." In order to respond to a situation that measures intellectual ability, a person must use abilities that are not usually considered "intellectual." The person must be able to see, hear, read, write, speak, move, or do something in order to manifest ability to accomplish tasks, solve problems, reason, use language, discern figures, or do whatever is required by a particular instrument which is used to measure intellectual ability. In fact, a person who is responding to a measure of intellectual ability is really using many abilities, but perhaps attention is being focused only on the so-called intellectual aspects of functioning because that functioning is under examination and not ability to move or speak, etc. Regardless of what the examiner might be focusing on, the examiner still considers the fact that all human abilities are related. The examiner considers that a person is a oneness which transcends or is more than the sum of those abilities. Thus, when we concern ourselves with human intellectual ability we are in reality focusing our attention on one description of how we interact with our environment. There are many descriptions, however; and the various arts and sciences which try to understand and express humanity describe us in many different ways, as we have already mentioned.

Using what ideas have been developed, let us now consider psychic ability in humans. Although there is no "Psi-Q" as such, detection and measurement of psychic ability have been carried out for years. That someone will someday index psychic ability, as intellectual ability has been indexed, and will make a mathematical ratio of pertinent factors, is simply a matter of time. Once the scientific community realizes more fully the potential in humanity and comes to awareness that humanity has vast areas of ability yet to be explored, we will probably have a "Psi-Q" index comparable to the I.Q. index. Our subjective education will then have come of age. That is what Mind Control Method is all about. Mind Control Method is our educating ourselves subjectively.

As you might expect, psychic ability can be expressed in various ways. And like intellectual ability, psychic ability has many other abilities hidden within it. Psychic ability really represents our ability to interact with our environment, but in ways that are somewhat different from the ordinary five-senses kind of commerce. We ordinarily see with our eyes, but if we are deprived of our eyes, then we "see" with our fingers, ears, and total body responses. In other words, deprive us of our eyes and we sense our environment in ways other than the person with unimpeded vision. In like manner, a person senses the environment psychically, with no interference by time and space barriers. There is psychic vision; it is called <u>clairvoyance.</u> There is psychic hearing which is called <u>clairaudience.</u> There are also psychic tasting, touching, smelling; they are all called <u>clairsentience.</u> As you can understand, what you call the experience is really determined by your point of view. If you are describing visualization and imagery, you will speak of clairvoyance. But since psychics do not experience imagery all the time, you need terms to describe their other experiences. Clairsentience and clairaudience are adequate for general purposes. These three terms describe the mode or way of experiencing. Thus, a psychic experience can be described in terms of how it is received or sent. Receiving-sending sounds is clairaudience; receiving-sending feelings is clairsentience.

Now that we have introduced a process, namely sending and receiving, we are discussing psychic ability in a wider dimension. Because we have changed our point of view, we need more terminology. Psychic ability can also be described as ability to send and receive images, sounds, and feelings other than by the five-senses. If you turn your attention to the sending-receiving aspects, then you will need terms like <u>telepathy</u> and <u>thought transference</u>. Both terms describe the relationship of two or more people in contact with one another psychically. When someone in the relationship sends communications (feelings, sounds, or images), and knows he is sending to someone who is aware of receiving those communications, the process is termed "telepathy." When parties in the relationship send or receive, but may or may not be aware of sending or receiving, the term "thought transference" is used. PK (psychokinesis) is simply another form of thought transference. Typically, instances of mind influencing matter over spatial distances is a form of sending and receiving. The energy of mind is focused, laser like, and influences objects, persons, etc., in a sending-receiving relationship. We need the term "PK" to describe a particular energy transfer from sender to receiver in such a situation.

Let us shift our attention now and consider sending and receiving images, sounds, and feelings across barriers of time, such as past or present. The terms <u>retrocognition</u> and <u>precognition</u> refer to these time-aspects of psychic experience. If the psychic experience deals in the past as such, it is said to be "retrocognition;", whereas, if the psychic experience relates to the future of persons, things, or events, as such, the experience is called "precognition." Both types of experience transcend barriers of time and the psychic is able to manipulate the experience regardless of time. In a manner of speaking, time is held constant and is controlled as a factor of the experience.

Without going on and on to the point of tedium, let us summarize by saying that we can be viewed several ways; our experience can be described from various points of view. If we describe our experience in terms of intellectual functioning, we refer to intellectual ability. When we treat our experience in terms of psychic functioning, we refer to psychic ability. I. Q. is an index of measured intellectual functioning; "Psi-Q" is a possible index of measured psychic functioning. But both indices refer to our measured ability and experience. Humanity is able in all its abilities to interact with the environment. Sometimes that environment is experienced at the Beta level of brain wave frequencies, and sometimes at the Alpha or Theta levels.

When we function at Inner Conscious Levels and process information at those dimensions, we subjectively communicate. Some people like to call such functioning psychic, to distinguish it from physical, but it is easy to understand that it is still people processing information to solve problems through communication which is nothing more than a form of interaction with the environment. It all depends on whether we use our periscope or our sonar, or both.

How do we learn to use our sonar? Here it is that the Mind Control Lecturer at an opening lecture will discuss how you develop your Mind Control principles and techniques by means of the Silva Method. And that brings us to the next chapter.

4

How you develop your Mind Control Method

As I sat and listened to Jose Silva discuss what the program was about, little did I realize that I would be one among hundreds of Mind Control Lecturers who would one day be previewing the basic series for opening lecture participants. Since that warm night in August, 1968, literally hundreds of lecturers have gone forth in the United States, Mexico, Canada, the United Kingdom, Central and South America, Europe, the Middle and Far East, Africa, Australia, and plans are now being made for all worldwide points where human beings find themselves. The man has duplicated himself many times and the Silva Method now extends to all points of our globe under the guidance of qualified and certified lecturers who make up Silva Mind Control International, Inc., or Mind Control, Inc.

The Institute of Psychorientology, Inc., the founding

organization, has continued to be the family center of all the corporations and manages Research and Development, training of lecturers, and all of the copyrights, trademarks, service marks, etc., but has turned over much of its function to Silva Mind Control International, Inc. The thousands of graduates are continually serviced by Silva Sensor Systems, a division which operates the Mind Control Book Store and offers tapes and various Mind Control Trainers. Since continuing service to graduates entails providing developmental guidance for continuing education and research, Psychorientology Studies International, Inc. was assigned the task of serving graduates. What was originally the Laredo Parapsychology Foundation brought forth Psychorientology Studies International, Inc., as it has come to be known. Through this international body graduates keep Beta contact with each other, share research techniques and findings, sponsor speakers, and benefit from continuing education through special seminar activities and workshops. The organization is directed by James Needham, an officer in several of the above mentioned corporations, and one of the veteran Mind Control graduate researchers and lecturers.

It is soon quite obvious to opening lecture participants that Silva Mind Control Lecturers are presenting a time-honored and well-researched system: The Silva Method. It has been brought to the public as a service which students support and enthusiastically recommend to their friends, even before they have graduated themselves. When I took the Basic Series, there were eight weeks between units. You will remember that I had first heard of the Basic Series in June but was not allowed to enroll until August. The reason was that Jose was the only lecturer in the entire U.S. at that time and his commitments were spread out all over cities in Texas. Now, incoming students can complete the work in a week! If they choose to, they may take the series in sequence, waiting between units as time and convenience might dictate. But whether they take the 40-48 hours in a week or two, or wait a month between units, they are still successful upon graduating. The Silva Method is so versatile, as research has demonstrated, that it can be tailored to fit any group or circumstance; the only requirement is that the student be able to communicate in a classroom type situation. We have graduates as young as 8 and as old as 108! Age is not a barrier. And there are special courses for youth and for business executives. As we develop more, lectures are being specialized for various professional disciplines also, such as doctors, chiropractors, lawyers, engineers, etc.

Mind Control Method is versatile because it is you using your ability under your own self-controlled sense of awareness according to a valid and reliable system of programming end-results for problem solving. The Silva Method helps you help yourself and help others to help themselves. It sits in any pew in any church; it rallies around any flag; it shouts "Hurrah!" in any political arena; it goes where you go, because it is you using your own abilities, but so much more effectively than you ever have! If you are not comfortable in church, in your business, in your home, or with yourself, then you use your Mind Control Method to make yourself comfortable. You have a Kingdom within you — and you can learn to enter that Kingdom, learn the laws that you can apply, and everything you need comes. And that's a fact. Everything! It only takes time to manifest what you want. Your desire, belief, and expectancy are the key factors, as you will come to learn in the Basic Series. And you will learn how to trigger them and apply them in such a way that you get to the desired level of mind that triggers the proper frequency for communication.

But how do we go about developing our Mind Control Method? "Simply," replies the Mind Control Lecturer.

You start with MC101CR (Controlled Relaxation), the unit we all begin with. It is approximately 10 hours: your opening lecture, and eight additional hours of lecture work. You go through a well-paced routine of lectures, discussions, breaks for relaxation, question and answer periods, and mental training exercises which you will come to know as programming or conditioning cycles. We work in groups, but everyone gets the individual attention he needs, as in any classroom situation. In the conditioning cycles you actually learn how to enter your Kingdom and you learn how to program points of reference which give you self-control so you can do it all for yourself. You learn the techniques in such a way that you can help yourself from the start. Each time that you leave class you will have learned applications that are practical and that you can use immediately. Besides learning how to enter and exit from your Kingdom, in MC101CR you learn how to relax yourself at will, and how to use that relaxation to wipe out needless anxiety and to challenge needless fears. Why shouldn't you use your Mind Control Method to go through your day successfully and happily? We are all called to success, not failure; to hopefulness, not fearfulness. And we learn how to use those newly self-managed levels of mind to make more effective decisions: personal, family, business, or whatever our concern. Applying your Mind Control Method, as you will come to realize, is really limited only by the limits on your creative ingenuity. Whether our problems be in education, religion, business, health or politics, whether they be personal, family, or societal, we can devise applications to help solve those problems.

During the last four hours of MC101CR, you begin to program problem-solving techniques like Sleep Control—how to go to sleep naturally, without the need for drugs—and get a normal night's rest and awaken refreshed at your proper time. You see, drugged sleep can be harmful sleep. Drugs tend to deprive us of needed variation in sleep levels; the drugs tend to lock us in certain frequencies to the loss of others, not to mention the extra burden put on the body to metabolize chemistry that it did not need. It is a thought similar to those developed in Chapter 3 where we discussed our creating needless dependencies. And if you want to awaken without the need for an alarm clock, or remain awake without the need for chemical stimulants, you can apply Awake and To Awaken Control that you learn in MC101CR. You learn the basic principles of programming that allow you to control your own behavior in these areas. Think of staying awake naturally as you press on in your journey when you are traveling and feel you cannot stop for sleep. You need not be a menace to yourself or others on the highway and you need not drug yourself. And if you are studying for an exam or trying to finish your brief, or whatever, but you simply do not take time for sleep, you do not need to "pop a pill" to stay awake. Simply use your Awake Control formula-type technique. It works!

Did you ever suffer a headache, either migraine or tension type? If so, you will especially appreciate the Headache Removal Control techniques you learn in this basic 101 unit. There is not very much that current laboratory research has uncovered about removing headaches. Typically advertising tells you to take one type of medication or another. Scientists have been known to throw their hands up in relative desperation over the migraine situation. There is just not much they know to do for it, even after years of researching. Well, you will learn not only how to rid yourself of such conditions but how to prevent them from coming on! A wild claim? Indeed not. As we will share with you in the next chapter, this very application of Mind Control Method is so effective that it attracted the attention of a major university medical school because of its effectiveness. But your Lecturer will hasten to counsel that you always work under the guidance of your health caretaker in matters of health. Seek help whenever you feel you need it; and remember that pain has survival value to the extent that it signals something that we ought to look into.

Another problem-solving application you will learn in MC101CR is the Dream Control technique. That's right. You can control your dreams. You say you do not even remember dreams? Well your first step in applying this formula is to learn how to recall dreams. In MC101CR you learn how to do just that. We all dream. As we discussed in Chapter 2, if we did not dream we would not stay healthy very long. Sleep and dream research has demonstrated that fact. We're pretty healthy, goes the general statement, so we must be dreaming. If we did not dream, we would show poor emotional control, have physiological fatigue, and we would have slowness, even impairment, of thought processes. But not only do we dream, we can also influence the content of dreams. You are right—yours and others' dreams! That being a fact means that you can trigger a dream to help you solve a problem. You can then use your time more effectively. Why waste time during the day on a problem you can solve at night while you sleep? Einstein used the dream approach, as did Bohr, Leer and others. And how often have you read in both sacred and secular scriptures that "a vision came to him while he slept," etc.? "Welcome aboard," says the Mind Control Lecturer; "you, too, can tap your creative potential."

After completing MC101CR you are prepared to go on to MC202GSI – the General Self-Improvement unit. It builds on what you learned in 101, and it takes you into programming in a very practical way. Since we will discuss programming in Chapter 6, we will defer discussion of it as such. But let us look at the techniques you learn to apply in 202.

You learn to locate your mental screen, that area of mind projection where you visualize, imagine scenes, image things in daydreaming, etc. The Lecturer will then help you learn to use it by sharing techniques for claiming your good memory. You know that no one has a bad memory. All memories are good. And you will learn a system for improving use of yours. It is based on association and the ability to get to a proper level of mind to impress and recall information. And you will learn the Three-Fingers Technique for problem solving with a very useful application in Test Taking. Never again will you have to hand in an unanswered question or a blank test!

As you learn to use the Mirror Of The Mind Technique, you will really feel thankful that Mind Control Method came your way. It is probably the most popular problem solving technique among Mind Control practitioners. You will learn how to use your mirror approach to change problems to solutions, illness to health, poverty to abundance, hate to love — you learn how to image end-results that you desire and expect. In other words, you have a practical tool to "Pray, believing you have received; to ask, knowing you have accomplished." And you can use it to help others, too! We will share a powerful story in the next chapter about a mother who helped her son when she applied her Mirror of the Mind Technique. You will find it inspiring.

Since all of your experience is worth cultivating, and because you want to awaken all of your vast and resourceful Kingdom within, you learn Hand Levitation and Glove Anesthesia techniques also. You learn how to program your body to respond to the guidance of your mind. In fact, you learn how to reverse psychosomatic illness to psychosomatic health by learning principles of body-mind unity. And as researchers like Dr. Alfred Cantor have found, over 80% of illnesses are psychosomatic--meaning that mental and/or emotional causes bring on the illness. In MC202GSI you learn how to help yourself claim the health we are all called to. And you also learn Weight and Habit Control--principles you can apply to any personal concerns you have of your own well-being. You learn how to supplement good health-management programs, like dieting and exercising, with programming at effective levels of mind so that you become the person you want to be under your own self-control.

But before you finish 202, you also learn another popular problem-solving technique: The Glass of Water Technique. How to solve problems at night while you sleep by putting them on a glass of water. And it, too, works! Put as many problems on that glass of water as you can keep track of. Expect results and you get them, because it is you helping yourself. You find information within yourself of your mind searches out the information wherever it can be found.

In 202 you have been learning how to project your mind. Because of this, you are now ready to go on to MC303ESP. ESP? That is right. But not "Extra-sensory perception." In Mind Control Method, we say <u>Effective Sensory Projection</u> because we know there is nothing "extra" about it--everybody has the ability. It is more than perception because you are able to project beyond what the five-senses perceive, and you actually participate actively and passively in the process. In 303 you establish points of reference that enable you to project your inner senses and get information at various levels and depths of the different kingdoms called mineral, vegetable and animal. You also design and build a working laboratory at this creative dimension that gives you all the information, tools, and assistance that you could ever need. You actually go within, create imageful expression of your Kingdom, and start functioning creatively in that Kingdom at the new-found subjective level for problem solving. You start learning some of the laws that prevail in that Kingdom and how to apply them for effective functioning. Actually, in MC303ESP you really actualize your potential for subjective communication by subjectively educating yourself. You have now arrived and are now claiming your rightful heritage; and because of your having established controlled points of reference, you can use your heritage in a functional way.

Throughout the basic series you have cultivated your inner senses that we discussed in Chapter 3, and you have awakened your imagination, thereby opening the doorway into the psychic or spiritual realms. In MC303ESP you begin to use that doorway, and you enter the subjective world of reality. Reality? That's right, R E A L I T Y ! Reality is all that is, and the subjective levels at which you learn to function are real. As you have outer senses, so you have inner senses, as we discussed in Chapter 3. You awaken your inner senses when you function at Inner Conscious Levels. Your imagination, which you used in Chapter 3 when you recalled the last meal you had had and re-experienced eating and drinking that meal, enables you to experience directly at other than the five-senses or physical dimension. And you actually develop and learn to control your imagination in 303.

"But how do I know I am dealing with reality as such and not fiction?" you might ask. Simply because you can test the reality of inner sensing and the reality of imagination and know it is fact.

Let us suppose you are a scientist who is accustomed to testing the factualness of things, how would you go about testing the reality of inner sensing and imagination? You would go the direct route or the indirect route; there are no other possibilities. The direct route is to experience for yourself. That is the way you find out if the weather is cool enough for a sweater or jacket--you simply open the door and let the air hit you. Accordingly as you feel comfortable or chilly you either reach for more clothes or you do not. Your own immediate experience is about the best test for the reality of anything. You may misinterpret what you experience, or you may fail to communicate the experience accurately or totally, but that you are immediately experiencing is undeniable. Because immediate experience is self-evident it truly transcends proof. It is the only time you experience reality with the probability statement of 1.0 or unit probability. All else in probability statements attempts to approach that unit probability. You will enjoy this unit probability of the reality of "inner sensing" and imagination when you work cases in MC404AESP, the last segment of your Mind Control Basic Lecture Series or you can get your money back. In fact, some students experience of inner sensing long before completion of the 404. But we will discuss MC404AESP when we have completed this discussion about subjective reality.

So, you can test for yourself whether or not subjective sensing deals with fact; before you graduate, you will be certain that you can subjectively communicate and get real information that helps you solve real problems. You will know that the subjective level deals with reality. But what about proving to others that inner sensing and imagination are real? You can do that too. But to do it, you go the indirect route. It is the route of indirect experience. You could invite a skeptic or one who is looking for proof, to a graduate meeting where graduates could demonstrate the reality of subjective communication. That would be what scientists would call an ecological or natural experiment. The natural scientists who observe plants, animals, and people in their natural surroundings with no intentional or deliberate control on the researcher's part that might interrupt the natural processes in any way are conducting a natural experiment. They subsequently attempt through mathematically precise means to analyze the data and discover lawful relationships for prediction. That is what science and the scientific method are all about. Were an outsider to witness graduates working problem cases, using the Silva Method of subjective communication, the outsider would be like the scientist observing phenomena and discovering lawful relationships.

A more indirect approach would be to have the observer ask the graduates if they can by means of subjective communication truly experience reality. The observer would then be taking their word for it, but it can be a valid and reliable source of evidence. For example, courts of law use this type of witnessing to reconstruct a crime, whether felony or misdemeanor. Did the red car hit the blue car? Did the blue car stop for the stop sign? Was the red car speeding? And so forth. What do the witnesses say? Accordingly as the testimony approaches unit probability in a rather imprecise way the court makes its decision. Your belief that the American Revolution and the fall of the Roman Empire are facts of history is dependent on such similar witnessing. The truthfulness and authority of the witnessing testimony are the critical factors in your decision to attest or not to the reality witnessed to. Library shelves are filled with such evidence for the reality of much which you hold as fact. And many of the so-called facts stored in your brain cell impressions are dependent on such indirect proof. But simply taking the graduates' word for it may not satisfy your need for proof because it removes you too far from the experience itself. Is there another method of proof?

Yes, another kind of experiment called the "laboratory" experiment. That is the type that scientists get very excited about because they can control the factors, either by direct manipulation or by statistical means. You see, when scientists can control factors then they believe what they experience is fact. Accordingly as others can duplicate their findings by manipulating the same variables and continue to approach unit probability sufficiently when the data are analyzed, they feel that their conclusions are validly and reliably stated. On such verified hypotheses systems and theories are predicated and on predictable findings laws are founded. And when scientists deal with lawfulness, they are happiest.

Jose Silva is such a scientist. He, too, wanted to know if inner sensing and imagination were real. Here is what he designed to investigate the facts. He trained two youngsters, Jimmy and Timmy, using the Silva Method, to enter subjective levels of mind and remain there to work problems with self-controlled awareness. They were able to communicate at subjective levels, in other words. He used youngsters, as we said in Chapter 2, because they tell it "like it is" and they are relatively unbiased when compared to adults. He also wanted subjects who were as naive as possible, lest their sophistication contaminate the experiment. And lest he contaminate the experiment by what he thought he engaged two other experimenters. Experimenter #1 was in a room with Jimmy and Experimenter #2, in a separate and removed room with Timmy. At a certain point in time, Jose told both Experimenters to instruct their subjects to enter their subjective levels of mind. Then Jose told Experimenter #1, who was with Jimmy, to have his subject create something in his imagination; anything would do. At the same time Jose told Experimenter #2 to have his subject, Timmy, enter his subjective level of mind and find out what Jimmy was doing. Jimmy indicated to his experimental control what he was doing; namely, "I'm making a little truck; it has a green body and red wheels," he said. In the distant room Experimenter #2 asked Timmy what Jimmy was doing. "Oh, he's making a little toy truck." "Well, describe it," said Experimenter #2. "Oh, it has a green body and red wheels," replied Timmy.

That experiment has since been replicated, with many such Timmys and Jimmys. In fact, many graduates duplicate with other type phenomena. The design proves that imagination is so real that others can experience it directly. It proves that thought transference is fact also at the subjective level, not only the objective. It proves that inner sensing deals with fact, imagined or physically palpable. How many Timmy's concentrically witnessing to a fact would you take as valid and reliable evidence for the existence of that fact? How many do you demand in your courts of law, or your archives of history, or your experimental laboratories? You see, scientists eventually stop testing for themselves and begin to take the reports of others for granted, as long as the statistical analyses are up to the current coefficient of acceptability. Scientists start accepting things on faith; that is, faith in their fellow professionals and faith in their methods. And isn't that what we have all done, if we believe that astronauts have walked on the moon; if we believe that heart and other organ transplants are now possible; if we believe that America is both North and South, and North America broke from a mother country at one time? It was called the American Revolution last we heard or read.

So, Mind Control Method invites you to widen your understanding of reality. It is more than meets the objective five senses. Reality is all that is, and you can be aware of much more of what is when you turn on your inner senses and tune in. You can solve so many more problems because you can get so much more information, if you apply the Silva Method and use your abilities for subjective communication. That is what you will be doing in MC404AESP. AESP stands for Applied Effective Sensory Projection. And that is exactly what you do. In 404 you learn to apply your subjective level of mind to solve problems. We start perfecting ourselves on a level of deep concern to everyone on this planet: the human condition. We know that there are basic human needs that we will do well to satisfy before we can hope to accomplish any uplifting on this planet. And one of the most basic is health, physical and psychological. So we detect problems in health and we correct those problems, all at a subjective level, in order to help people who are not physically present or in our environment. The people can be prisoners in Vietnam, or citizens in Paris, France, or Los Angeles, California, U.S.A. As you learn in your Mind Control Basic Lecture Series, Time and Space are not the barriers at the subjective level that they seem to be to the five-senses. And this whole process of psychic investigation we call <u>Psychorientology</u>: Science of Mind Control, or Science of Self-Guidance. It is the science of the future today and your means of taking steps into the second phase of human evolution on this planet. Welcome aboard for an exciting uplift, not only for yourself and your loved ones, but for all of humanity.

It is called the Silva Method and it works!

5

By your fruits you shall know


When we discussed Headache Removal Control in the last chapter, we asked if you thought that learning how to rid yourself of such discomforting conditions as tension and migraine headaches was a wild claim, particularly if you can also prevent those conditions from coming on. And we mentioned that it was just such a claim that occasioned our sponsoring research at a major university. The story is an interesting one.

San Antonio, Texas, developed increasingly well as a Mind Control City. Ray Glau, (who was formerly one of the most successful franchisees and lecturers of the Silva Method but who has since become a Vice-President with Silva Mind Control International, Inc.), has guided development in that city for over three years and one of the notable achievements that he, lecturers, and graduates accomplished was to establish a very successful Silva Mind Control Center.

Graduates met nightly for constructive Mind Control projects in such areas of concern as stock market investment, health cases, criminology, finding lost persons and objects, general self-improvement through tapes and reading, language study, and so forth. In addition, the Mind Control Basic Lecture Series were held at the Center regularly and word had spread throughout the area with the result that more and more people went to the Center and enrolled in classes to help themselves through the Silva Method.

Our story concerns three such people who enrolled in the Mind Control Basic Lecture Series in San Antonio. Without telling anyone that they were patients of psychiatrists in the area, they took MC101CR. Their specific complaint, as we later learned, was that they suffered from migraine headaches. Since their doctors had been unable to help them get rid of the conditions, and since their doctors had heard reports from the Mind Control students that they had been able to rid themselves of the headaches they had been having, the doctors sent them to take the course work, sort of as test cases. "Why not," they must have thought, "let them get help wherever they can, if we cannot help them!" Not only did the three rid themselves of their painful conditions, but they also learned how to prevent such attacks in the future. They learned how to use preventative Mind Control techniques. And, as usual, the Lecturer counseled the participants to work carefully in health matters with the guidance of their health caretakers.

When the patients made reports to their physicians, the doctors were so impressed that they arranged that Jose Silva be invited to talk to a group of staff members and students at a university in Texas, a school of medicine. As they informed him, the group was interested in learning what his method was doing to accomplish such things. They also requested that there be some sort of demonstration so that they could record the brain waves of a subject during the demonstration. Jose agreed and took one of his sons, Antonio, as a test subject. Since Jose had begun research by using his own children as subjects, what could be more fitting than that he follow that pace-setting precedent upon this occasion?

Jose Silva's talk and demonstration and Antonio's EEG recordings taken by the Department of Psychiatry at the university on November 7, 1970, while Antonio worked a project at his subjective level were so impressive that: 1) Silva Mind Control International, Inc., funded research at a second university in Texas in the area of feedback psychophysiology, including brain wave analysis and feedback using Mind Control trained subjects as experimental groups. This research came about because the experimenter on the staff of the second university was a participant in that lecture and demonstration; and 2) many more research projects have subsequently been designed.

Antonio Silva's working a case before a small group of interested scientists may well be the most publicized case of all Mind Control history. If it aroused academia and the scientific community out of its lethargic and ultra-conservative posture in relation to subjective communication it may well have been one of the most effective. Only time will tell.

Mind Control Method has quite a history of effective and successful problem solving. There is the narrative about the waiter who became a true servant of humanity. To meet this man is to meet a humble, loving person who feels a burning desire to help his fellow human beings. He was a waiter at a restaurant in Laredo, Texas, when he met Jose Silva. He was earning under $20.00 per week at his job. He studied with Jose in some of the research prior to 1966 and was so enthusiastic about his abilities developed by means of the Silva Method that he began to practice working on psychic cases to help people heal themselves of illnesses and problems. As he specialized his application of the Mind Control Method he became quite expert, and quite popular. Eventually he gave up his job in Laredo, took up full-time residency in Mexico and simply helped as many people as might request his help, the way Edgar Cayce used to.

Our one-time-waiter-turned-servant never had to ask for money—he was supported entirely by generous donations. In fact, many people would reward him only with a rich "Thank you." But other people of means would more than make up for any deficit in the bookkeeping necessities of life. You see, this Mind Control graduate walked that extra mile. People would write in to request his help on a certain matter and he would help them solve their problem. But he also helped them get rid of those problems which they failed to mention. When he replied through his secretary that he had worked for them, and that he also worked on "those headaches you've been having," they would be so grateful that they would reply in equally generous coinage. It is rather obvious why we call him "Our waiter who became a true servant of humanity."

And then there is Evelia Calderon, a petite raven haired Spanish miss, who lives in Mexico. My first encounter with her was when my wife and I were studying Mind Control Method; Jose brought Evelia in to demonstrate for us, as Lecturers occasionally do bring experienced graduates in. I will never forget her working about 10 cases in about two hours. We were amazed at how accurate she was in detecting health problems about people whose names we gave her. When you give only the name, age and location of your father to a Mind Control graduate and the graduate proceeds to describe his health complaint in accurate detail as a medical doctor might have diagnosed it, you gasp somewhat in amazement. When that same graduate then proceeds to send help at the subjective level to your father who is living in another state, you wipe the tears away from your eyes. And all is straightforward. The graduate talks to you and even keeps her eyes open sometimes! In fact, some graduates become so expert at entering subjective levels that you can hardly detect it. Only the trained observer can tell.

"But do the graduates cause the person to get better?" is the typical question asked of lecturers who share such Mind Control experiences with inquiring people. And usually the Lecturer answers by sharing more experiences. Desire, belief, and expectancy on the sender's and the receiver's parts are important casual factors. As the graduate generates desire to help someone and energizes expected end-results and sends or "thinks" those perfect end-results to the person being worked on subjectively, the graduate takes it for granted that the work will be effective. To doubt is to throw up a needless barrier that can cause failure. The graduate presumes the work is effective unless negative feedback indicates the need to work more, change perspective, or leave it in the hands of a higher intelligence than the graduate has developed. Feedback that indicates that the graduate has been helpful is a positive cybernetic. And the results can be very rewarding.

Positive reward was what came to a Mind Control mother in Lubbock, Texas. She had just completed MC202GSI in which you learn the Mirror Of The Mind Technique. After she had returned home and was retiring, her young son began his rather usual asthmatic breathing. She could hear him plainly although he was in his own room down the hall. At that moment, the mother altered her level of consciousness and from her subjective level of mind that she learned to control through the Silva Method, she began to talk to her son as though he were physically present before her. He still lay in his bed, however. She had generated a strong desire to help her son and she expected results. In fact, she challenged the Silva Method by thinking, "Well, if this really works I should be able to help my son." After a few moments of mentally projecting healing thoughts toward her son, she noticed that she heard nothing. She leapt from her bed and ran quietly to her son's room. He was breathing normally! She was amazed.

She kept her amazement to herself and told no one in class about it. Eight weeks or so later when classes were in session she shared the good news. But she added, "You know, he hasn't breathed asthmatically since then. And you know what? I don't think he will breathe asthmatically again!" To follow this story up a fellow graduate inquired as to the outcome about two years later. The child had had only one relapse that centered around an emotional conflict with a teacher. The Mind Control mother promptly worked subjectively on her son and made contact with the teacher. The condition was cleared and the problem was solved.

Yes, the graduates can add energy to help the person get rid of the problem. If you want to call that "causing the person to get better" you can. In any event, Mind Control Method works. Try it!

About this time opening lecture participants begin to wonder if the Silva Method only works in matters of health. The lecturer reminds them that we consider the human condition in health matters an appropriate place to begin to develop our abilities to help ourselves and help others help themselves, but we can apply our Mind Control Method in many ways.

Did you know that graduates can sense problems in machinery? I remember one incident in Dallas, Texas. (If we talk a lot about Texas it is because it all began there and much of our research experience was gotten while lecturing there.) One of our graduates was called upon for help. It seems that a computer had broken down and the only man knowledgeable enough (they thought) to begin to look for the problem was out on the west coast looking after a similar model that needed attention. So our graduate went to his Level, as we say, and sensed clairvoyantly that the problem was in a certain section, about two panels down, and so forth. The Mind Control graduate knew virtually nothing about repairing computers, but he was able to describe what the problem and problem area were with such accurate detail that the computer people were able to locate the faulty part, repair it, and in short order. Think of the time, money, and personnel you can save, if you train your computer scientists, whether in software or hardware, with the Silva Method. In fact, we say that the least you can do with your Mind Control Method is much more than you could do before. If you have not subjectively educated yourself you have not yet completed your education, no matter how many D.C., D.D., Ph.D., or M.D. degrees you might have taken.

We have graduates who examine their automobiles and airplanes at a subjective dimension now whenever they sense that something needs repairing. Did you ever take your car in for service or mechanical repairs and wonder, "Did they fix it?" Why bother yourself with poor service? Simply tell them what it is that needs repairing — they'll be asking you when there will be a Mind Control series for mechanics!

There is this Mind Control graduate who is a commercial pilot with a large airline. He is one of many. He now uses his Mind Control Method to sense his equipment before he takes it off the ground. If he detects any problem, he instructs the ground crew to check it out. His guiding ethic is: "Why take unnecessary risks with beautiful lives and expensive equipment when I can take a few moments at my Level and check out my ship to avoid such loss?" And Mind

Control graduates have been known to help cars operate successfully for more than a week when repairs were needed much sooner than they could be made. On one occasion a graduate seemed to be the factor that kept an accident from happening.

She saw clairvoyantly that a friend's car was going to break down and that there was going to be an accident. She worked at her level and sent subjective communication to the friend to take the car in and have it checked because of the noise that was going to develop. The noise developed, the friend took the car in and the mechanic announced that one of the wheels should have come off because bolts were almost sheared. He could not understand what kept the wheel on. There was no accident. Only our graduate was the wiser about the whole situation. Graduates don't usually go around saying, "I'm helping you." But they do help. It is kind of a quiet mission. Maybe you have been helped and did not realize it. Be thankful anyway.

Do you know that doctors, lawyers, judges, nurses, teachers, homemakers, children students, engineers, psychologists, and many, many other professionals and non-professionals have learned how to use the Silva Method to help make this a better world to live in so that when we move on we can leave a better world for those who follow? You will be in good company when you choose to become a Mind Control graduate.

There was also the graduate who used Mind Control Method to keep better discipline in her classroom of fifth graders. Even the music teacher commented that her class was the most well behaved—and so enthusiastic as students! Can you imagine a classroom of youngsters (and oldsters) who have learned the Silva Mind Control Method? The teachers would really have to be on their toes, so to speak, to keep them challenged. At this writing, there are many projects in schools (primary and secondary levels), colleges and universities. Pilot programs have been conducted. Faculties have been trained in the Silva Method and students have gone through Mind Control series as part of their elective and required curricula. We are looking forward to the day when Mind Control Method will be available in all school systems and universities. But if all parents train their own children in the Silva Method, then it will eventually be learned in the home. And that is where it ought to begin anyway. Every mother and father can learn how to train their own. As we will discuss in Chapter 6, after you have had the Mind Control Graduate Lecture Series, MC1001GLS, you will be able to work with your loved ones who are dependent on you for guidance. After all, if you don't work with your own, someone down the street will program them. Which do you prefer?

To continue our discussion, let us examine what is probably one of the most dramatic cases in Mind Control tradition. It is the case of the released prisoner of war. Graduates in the Panhandle of Texas are to be credited with this one. That is where Jose first taught classes in English, you remember. It seems that one student had received a report that her husband was missing in action over a war-torn area. She wondered if graduates could find out if he was all right and what might have happened to him. Jose directed the project and graduates uncovered information about the downed pilot's state of health, whereabouts, and so forth. The pilot's wife then asked when she would know for sure. Graduates worked again and precognitively experienced his date of return to this country subsequent to his release with two other prisoners of war. All came about as they had foreseen!

After his return to this country the pilot verified the Mind Control graduates' findings concerning his health, where he was kept a prisoner, etc. They were accurate in their detection of information and about solution of the problem of his release. Did they actually help in such a way that they were instrumental in his being released?

Accordingly as you answer that question you probably reveal your persuasion about the perfectibility of humanity. We can effect changes through energy that we manage from an Inner Conscious Level. We can send help to people even though they be at a distance. We can even change our environment with our Mind Control Method. Research our own graduates have done and the research of C. Backster demonstrate that thoughts influence plant life. And until we realize what our power of thought is capable of we will be neglecting the crucial element in solving our planet's ecological upset; our controlled sense of awareness is the key to solving all our problems. It has always been.

Seek the Kingdom within you, and work according to the lawful relationships that prevail there, and everything you need comes.

In other words, use your Mind Control Method!

6

Programming end-results


In case you are puzzling over the title of this chapter, let us clairfy the purpose we intend in the following pages of discussion. Because the Mind Control Graduate Lecture Series (formerly called Graduate Course) focuses on all the following topics:

1) Research and theories that preceded Mind Control Method;
2) Conditioning techniques out of which Mind Control Method was developed;
3) Using lower frequencies of brain in various applied fields such as Education, Business, Religion, Medicine, etc.;
4) Mind Control Method contrasted with so-called hypnosis;
5) Special conditioning for programming at deeper levels; and
6) The study of programming in general; namely, objective, objective-subjective, and subjective;

we will use the Mind Control Graduate Lecture Series as a

spring-board to discuss what programming and end-results are all about. As we discuss programming and end-results we will also be clarifying what we mean by subjective education.

We have already described <u>Psychorientology</u> or the Mind Control Method as a new science, the science of tomorrow today. As we proceed through the Basic Lecture Series MC101CR through MC404AESP, but most especially as we graduate from the Mind Control Graduate Lecture Series MC1001GLS, we understand that Psychorientology qualifies as a new body of scientific knowledge. <u>Psychorientology</u> is the result of years of careful research which investigated mind from a new perspective or dimension: the subjective level. For years the mind had either been denied or neglected in research using the scientific method, or it had been detected and measured almost out of existence in very narrow focus, such as in research at the Duke Parapsychology Laboratory, now defunct. When Jose Silva began researching the various hypotheses he had formulated through his years of study and observation he had already developed control of his own subjective levels. Basing new hypothesis-testing on his own personal experience of fact, he knew that the subjective level of mind was fact and could be developed and applied to problem-solving. It was with this persuasion that he began to train others and do research with children.

His methodology was precise and squared with the best standards of scientific method. As he blended his observations with certain assumptions he formulated hypotheses; he then tested those hypotheses. Accordingly as they were verified or not, he corrected his hypotheses and started over. He either replicated or revised, however the data dictated. Eventually his experimental designs became more standardized so that others could replicate. This generated new research which is manifest today, not only in the Silva Method as applied by all qualified and certified Lecturers, but in continuing new theoretical research, even at the university level in such areas as psychophysiological feedback. The current trend in biofeedback training is just a start by science to tap the kinds of applications for which people can use Mind Control Method. But rather than waste time (the problems on this planet are too vast and pressing to take needless detours!) on intermediate means and effects that are tangential to the method, Mind Control Method helps us turn the keys that unlock the hidden power that has lain dormant within us throughout years of scientific research: self-controlled levels of awareness. Controlling our own levels of awareness enables us not only to program our body functions (brain, so-called autonomic system, etc.) but also to set up such intelligent management of energy that we can program goals for ourselves and become the loving, self-fulfilled, and self-actualized persons we want to be. In addition, through our subjective education we learn subjective communication for solving problems by using information that we can get only at an inner level. We quickly learn to use all of our potential with greater precision and scope. Through practice and application of the principles and techniques we develop control of all our frequencies of brain so that our desire can tune us to any desired point of reference at any frequency of brain or level of mind, as we will discuss more at length in Chapter 7.

In becoming expert in <u>Psychorientology,</u> the practitioner uses the Silva Method to program self-control of points of reference at various levels of mind. This programming, in the best tradition of Pavlovian and present day behavior-therapy type conditioning, is one of the characteristic features that distinguishes the Silva Method from all the other approaches such as Zen, Buddhism, Transcendental Meditation, Yoga, Hypnotism, etc. The end-results of obtaining self-controlled sense of awareness for problem-solving, even at subjective levels of mind, when considered with the programming which is used in the Silva Method, are the distinguishing characteristics which make it unique. All other systems that come after it are founded upon it. Although there are some new uses for certain terms, Mind Control Method attempts to use concepts and terms that are already familiar to the students. It sees no need for unnecessary jargon. Scientists who indulge too freely in such word games frequently end up talking only to themselves.

Throughout all of its research Mind Control Method has focused on problem-solving; thus, it is an applied science as such. There is theory but only as it is relevant to solving problems. In fact, Mind Control Method is eminently applicable to all sorts of theoretical inquiry. In the field of parapsychological and metaphysical research, for example, many Psychorientologists are researching life before (reincarnation theory) and life after (survival theory) this present one we are given. Lecturers usually counsel, however, whenever the topics arise in class, that this present life that we are given should be our primary focus. What we do with this time and life is what truly matters, not what went before and what might come after. Solving problems effectively seems to be what we need to do. We have years of speculative theory that has not solved anything but vain curiosity at times. Such areas as reincarnation theory need much more research and we can use Mind Control Method to research them; we try, however, to focus in a pragmatic way on solving problems that abound on this planet of ours.

Because Jose Silva developed Mind Control Method by first using conditioning techniques found mainly in hypnotic research and because vestiges of those early techniques are still discernible in the Silva Method, it is not infrequent that lecturers and students get questions from people asking to know the differences between Mind Control Method and hypnosis. Some people even mistake hypnosis for Mind Control Method. Opening lectures and seminars are frequent occasions for some queries along that line. Lecturers even find that many people are somewhat frightened by the word "hypnosis." Although more research is being done in the field of therapeutics using hypnotic techniques, some investigators are researching the inadequacy of much of the previous research. One researcher in particular who is publishing more than some others is Theodore X. Barber. He is finding that subjects using imagination and suggestions are as effective sometimes as subjects in what researchers call hypnotic trance. The same type of phenomena can be produced, in other words, without hypnotic trance. You will probably find that Barber is doing transitional research that will bring him to Mind Control Method eventually. Let us hope so.

There are some people (even Mind Control students sometimes) who insist that Mind Control is hypnosis. Usually these are uninformed people who have not really investigated carefully. Typically, unprofessional people will be the first to level the many differences. But, then, we are trying to help people increase their awareness, so we should not be surprised that there are many who are not yet enlightened by facts. Let us consider some of the facts.

When Dr. James Braid first researched "nervous sleep" in the 19th century and coined the word "hypnosis," he apparently thought that the altered states of consciousness in his subjects were sleep states—his further research caused him to alter his assessment to neurypnology. But hypnosis as a concept and term had taken such hold that it has endured into present day research and popular literature. Actually, there is no such thing as _hypnosis_. The associated phenomena are not sleep states (_hypnos_ means _sleep_ in Greek) and research now indicates that these phenomena can be produced without the hypnotic rituals and techniques. As we in Mind Control Method know, altering a state of consciousness is positively correlated with altering brain frequencies, at least in the naive-like stages in the beginning. As the students advance, they can learn to alter their consciousness while there seems to be no detectable change in brain rhythms. In fact, some of our Mind Control adepts have puzzled scientists attempting to determine the frequencies at which the student's brain was functioning! As has always been the case, altering a state of consciousness, even in so-called hypnotic research, has never meant "going to sleep." Subjects in such research only go to sleep if they want to or need to.

To say that Mind Control Method is hypnosis is really to misunderstand the facts. Yoga, Transcendental Meditation, Zen, Buddhism, and Hypnotism are all different from each other, and they differ from Mind Control Method. Mind Control Method can be compared to a many-roomed mansion. Each of the approaches that seek to help a person alter focus of consciousness through natural means is but one room in the mansion. The Silva Mind Control Method is the most reliable, efficient, and practical method that systematizes altering states of consciousness naturally to solve problems. The other approaches are simply aspects of it.

The three distinguishing aspects of various approaches are: 1) Terminology, 2) Programming, and 3) End results. All three taken together make for differences among Yoga, Zen, Transcendental Meditation, Hypnotism, and so forth. Different end-results are really the critical areas where the differences manifest themselves. Simply changing terms and masking techniques do not really change anything substantially. The end-results in Mind Control Method of establishing points of reference to solve problems are truly unique and therefore distinctive in the Silva

Method.

Human beings have only one set of levels: levels of awareness that can be correlated with frequencies of brain wave activity. The levels are: Outer Consciousness, Inner Consciousness, and the so-called Unconsciousness. The brain frequencies are Beta, Alpha, Theta, and Delta, usually mixed, as scientists have been able to detect them and now classify them. Controlling sense of awareness at these frequencies is a phase of Mind Control Method. Using these controlled levels of awareness to solve problems is another. Being able to use subjective levels of mind to solve problems is one of the unique end-results attained through programming points of reference through the conditioning cycles. Such controlled sense of awareness is the fruit of the entire Mind Control process called subjective education, a new dimension in our leap forward on this planet. And it is a reliable and valid method.

Because Mind Control Method enables each individual student to control energy by intelligent self-management, the essential benefits found in the other approaches are open to the Mind Control adept. Practice is the only requirement after graduation. The principles and techniques are there in the Mind Control programming. And a lot of new jargon is not necessary. Mind Control Method can be expressed in all sorts of terminology: Business, Religion, Science, Philosophy, Theology--and even in Eastern or Western categories of thought! And all of these things are possible because the Silva Method helps individuals claim their own heritage of resourcefulness — that Kingdom-within which Jesus spoke of and taught, and that Buddha and Mohammed intimated. Entering the Kingdom and working according to lawful relationships that prevail therein enables the student to get everything needed — even control of body functioning so widely written of in biofeedback training research. But in Mind Control Method such benefits are automatic side effects and need not be focused on as such. They can be, if necessary--but the student graduate develops more and more control as needed.

But let us focus on so-called hypnosis as such, and point out some of the many differences. 1) In typical hypnotic research, the subject functions by suggestion primarily; he deals with information fed into him, so to speak, and typically only with that information. He rarely if ever assumes control to the point that he seeks information as an independent processing mind. In Mind Control Method the students are always independently accepting or rejecting, seeking more information, and so forth. Guided self-programming encourages the students to develop their own experiences and assume self-control from the beginning.

2) The hypnotic subject, depending on how much he has altered his level of consciousness, usually answers questions only. The Mind Control students answer and ask questions because they have controlled their levels of awareness in the process of altering those levels of consciousness.

3) In hypnotic research, the more the subject goes in the direction of Delta sleep, the more he tends to forget, and that rather automatically. Of course, he can be instructed to remember, and he can remember spontaneously also, with repeated training exercises. In Mind Control Method, the more students function with controlled awareness in Alpha and eventually in Theta levels, the more they remember. Awareness wipes out forgetting. In fact, the Mind Control students really discover the fact that we do not forget a thing when we can scan layers of brain cell impressions, so to speak.

4) In hypnotic investigation of deeply altered levels of awareness, the deeper the subject goes the more he surrenders controls and allows himself to be directed by an outside agent at Beta. In Mind Control Method, the more the stu-

dents established points of reference at the Alpha-Theta levels and the Inner Conscious Levels of functioning, the more they assume self-control, even over their so-called autonomic functioning.

All of the above differences are the result of the students' programming points of reference for themselves. As they establish these points of reference, they achieve more and more Mind Control functioning for the purpose of solving problems, especially through information gotten and processed at subjective levels of mind. Programming is a major difference, as we can understand. And programming self-control is of the essence.

Because of these outstanding differences, Mind Control Method is far superior. In addition, Mind Control students cooperate immediately, whereas in hypnotic research, it has been repeatedly reported that results are inconsistent because not all subjects cooperate. Sometimes the poor quality of the hypnotic operator is the causal factor, however. As has been said: there is no such thing as a poor subject, but there are poor hypnotic technicians.

And the end-result that seems to be most distinctive as far as students are concerned seems to be that Mind Control Method helps people help themselves. It may well be that this is a popular accomplishment among Mind Control students because the human mind does not like to be pushed around. It is rather the same thing that Perry London observed in his <u>Behavior Control</u>:

> Awareness is the instrument of control par excellence, replacing, in the advanced state it has achieved in human evolution, much of the biological armor that lower organisms use to battle for survival. The armamentarium of human invention, including modern technology, is an expression of the power placed in man's hands because of his great capacity for awareness. Until now,

his awareness has been directed at the things around him. Behavior-control technology has itself arisen from man's awareness of the relationship between his surroundings, his body parts, and his experiences of mood and thought, which he has labeled "mind." The solution to the problems of behavior control requires more focusing of human awareness on the subjective self, not to the exclusion of its surroundings, but for the expansion of its own contents. And there are no other solutions possible because there is no alternative to man's continuing to acquire knowledge, to build tools from it, and to use them. The only answer to man's increased general awareness is to increase his personal awareness. The only defense against the instrusions of science and technology, the cohorts of massed knowledge, is to expand and fortify his consciousness of self, the armor of individual knowledge. The only deterrent or reply to behavior control is to increase his technical mastery of his own behavior. Man's shield and buckler and, finally; his most potent weapon, is his individual power of awareness. It has always been. (Cf. London, page 215, in A select bibliography.)

Is it difficult to see how Mind Control Method is not only different from but far superior to hypnosis? Through Mind Control Method we claim our bedrock existence, and, regardless of Hamlet's puzzling, it is far better to be than not to be. Not only does Mind Control Method help us "be" but under our own self-control! We claim our human existence by becoming more personally aware. Then it is that we begin to perform human acts that help make this a better world in which to live.

In the Mind Control Graduate Lecture Series students also study the distinctions among various types of programming:

1) Objective, 2) Objective-Subjective, and 3) Subjective. Because Objective programming is the stuff of formal education as has been emphasized for years, the advanced Mind Control students turn their attention mainly to Objective-Subjective and Subjective types of programming. It is in this graduate series that they become reflective, about their formal subjective education as they began to develop it in MC101CR through MC404AESP, the basic series.

Objective programming is accomplished via the five senses while sender and receiver are functioning primarily at Beta frequencies of brain and are in each other's physical environment. Talking with a friend over coffee is a typical example. When either the sender or the receiver has altered levels of consciousness in the relationship, but is still in the physical environment of the other, we have a mixture of Objective and Subjective programming. This mixture occurs frequently in psychotherapy, psychoanalytic or otherwise. Probably therapy truly takes place only when there is communication at subjective levels. In hypnoanalysis, the analyst intentionally uses conditioning techniques to help the patient get to a subjective level so that regression or analysis can take place. The therapeutic use of altered states of consciousness for anesthetic purposes also employs Objective-Subjective type programming. Subjective programming, however, is communication and problem-solving that take place entirely at a subjective level. The sender is focusing the Inner Conscious Level and the receiver is not in the sender's physical environment; in addition, the receiver does not even have to be aware of being helped. The sender uses Beta, Alpha, and Theta levels accordingly as he or she needs to in order to solve the particular problem being focused on.

In subjective education, then, the Mind Control student

learns how to control levels of awareness, impress points of reference that give control at various levels of mind and frequencies of brain; and how to apply psychic energies for problem-solving in general and in particular. We discussed in Chapter 5 how some graduates are applying their Mind Control Method to satisfy various needs that arise. And we discussed various applications for standard techniques learned in the Mind Control Basic Lecture Series. In the Graduate Lecture Series the students learn how to use Theta functions of mind (Cf. Chart, page 93) both to help themselves and help others help themselves. The focus, however, is on helping others, especially loved ones, because the Mind Control students learn quite early in their study that the most effective way to help one's self is to help others help themselves, especially at the subjective level. As we shall see in the next chapter, however, we use whatever level we need to. We have established controls that enable us to vary levels simply by desiring. Our desire to help triggers the proper frequency. When we can control even Delta through practice we have attained Level 7—Cosmic Consciousness, Enlightenment, Self-Actualization — all that Christ Awareness has come to mean. Then we can do whatever needs to be done — we then will have arrived at the end of this earth plane mission.

7

The second phase of human evolution leads to the third

If becoming as childlike as quickly as possible is one of the goals of the Mind Control students, another of almost equal importance is cultivating the possible. With the sincerity, honesty, trust, and lively imagination of the child, the Mind Control students who allow themselves to entertain possibilities can program whatever they truly need, keeping in mind the principle, "It is not a matter of trying to get all you can; simply ask for and expect no less than you need." Once the graduates begin to apply the principles and techniques that they learned in the Mind Control series, and practice fortitude by sticking to their purposes, they start making changes that they desire. They improve their business, their health, their social relations, and even have a psychological cleansing if they feel that is what they need. Their creative use of their power within is limited only by their desire and expectancy.

The Mind Control graduates eventually realize that they create their own destiny by responsibly making decisions for themselves. Of course they get counsel and advice whenever they need it, because they recognize worthwhile help whenever they see it. And that they need help occasionally, they are the first to admit. But because of the Silva Method they have a new and reliable dimension of help for problem-solving and decision-making: Level 1. They have learned how to enter their Kingdom, and they are learning the laws that govern functioning there; accordingly as they function with increasing sense of self-controlled awareness at that inner dimension, they get everything they need. The more they are dependent on themselves, always working in a cooperative spirit of unity with others, the more they accomplish what they program. They have tapped the Source of all good, the Font of all energy. And they have found it all within themselves. The more they are dependent on factors outside of themselves to get what they need, the more time and energy it may take to accomplish their programming. The law that seems to be operating here is that law which governs the manifestation on earth of things done in the heavenly Kingdom. Time at the Outer Conscious Level and time at the Inner Conscious Levels are not perfectly correlated, as the Mind Control students learn in MC303ESP. Events can rush forward and backward in the inner Kingdom but they sometimes manifest very slowly at the outer dimension.

As you progress in your development through use of the Silva Method, you begin to change more and more toward fulfillment. You blend with the rhythmic ebb and flow of nature's cycling. As you make yourself more consciously one with all that is you begin to pulse with growth and stability patterns of energy flux. The deterioration that seems to claim so much of life and creative expression begins to vanish. It is as though the laws of material energy yield to higher laws of what is called spiritual energy. Just as the tree cycles through spring, summer, autumn, and winter, only to rise triumphant again in spring, so you begin to pulse with the vibrance of life, not death. You learn how to live and love life. But you are successful only to the extent that you allow your roots to sap up the energy from your source within.

Practicing through meditation is your way of keeping your tap root energetically supplied for life. Not tapping into your Source means death. That seems to be why scientists are finding that we need more than Beta activity at the brain frequency dimension. To remain healthy and to develop, we need variations within all four ranges of frequencies. As you alter your levels of mind by practicing, you automatically learn how to alter your brain frequencies. To be able to alter your frequencies at will is to be able to get what you need when you need it. Functioning at the Alpha-Theta dimensions as you do when you use your Inner Conscious Levels keeps you close to the stable processes of development. Decay eventually vanishes and death is no more. That you move on because of biological breakdown in body organs and processes is not your rightful heritage. As you partake in the childlike levels of mind, you automatically function at childlike frequencies of brain. And children grow and reach stability, don't they? Decay usually comes after the child has become a deteriorating adult. Keeping the body-mind unit in proper balance means letting intelligence manage and guide energy in a childlike way.

Learning how to go within to your Source is learning how to let intelligence manage without interference. Not only do you begin to experience reality as it truly is, but you begin to blend with it in a rhythmic balance of lawfulness. And lawfulness brings fulfillment because working within lawful relationships truly fees us. To "break the law" is to suffer the consequences. Ignorance is no matter; whether or not you know you "break the law," you still suffer. If you fall from a twenty-story building and you have not learned levitation and there is nothing to break your fall, the law of gravity still takes its toll. Because you know the law, however, you are more likely to avoid falling off twenty-story buildings. You are free of gravity only to the extent that you can first know its lawfulness and then operate within its scope or amend it because of higher controls. To know the law and function within it or rise above it because of higher controls is the function of awareness. And to the extent that you are aware you are free.

Everytime you enter Level 1, you are freeing yourself, healing yourself, helping yourself, automatically. Level 1 is your Kingdom-level within. You might liken the scale of consciousness to the descending scale of numbers 6 through 1. Level 6 is considered to be the Outer Conscious Level or Beta range of frequencies. You will study more in MC101CR how these levels are arrived at when you discuss entering and exiting from levels in your second 4-hour session. Level 6 is the world of the five senses and the world of action primarily. It is these levels where we often build up anxieties and tension and fatigue. In MC101CR we quickly learn how to counteract those needless blocks to good health and proper function by learning how to enter Level 1. As we alter our attention and focus at our Inner Level of awareness by the Silva Method, we arrive at Level 1 where we can function with full awareness and control, being able to come and go at will. Entering and exiting, after we have worked at Level 1 for whatever purpose, is a conditioning cycle. And you remember from Chapter 2 that a cycle is a completion from beginning to end of process. We begin our process of functioning at Level 1 by entering and we end by exiting. So, going from Level 6 to Level 1 and then back to Level 6 is a complete cycle.

Interesting things start to happen after we have practiced enough — and although the length of practice required is a very individual matter, 15 minutes at Level 1, three times a day, are suggested for excellent results. We gradually cause Level 1 to blend with all the other levels. We add Level 1 to Level 2 and Level 3, and so forth. When we have practiced to the extent that we have brought Level 1 into all our conscious levels then it is that we automatically blend whatever frequencies of brain that we need at a particular time. The function to be accomplished or the problem to be solved is what dictates the percentage of brain frequency we will use. If we need to be predominantly at Beta we are there. If Alpha is what we need most of, we are there.

When we become so expert that we can control even Delta with awareness, then it is that we leap forward into the third phase of human evolution on this planet, Level 7. We then will be controlling our entire Kingdom of possible dimensions. Delta, as we said in earlier chapters, is the region we are most ignorant of in our research. It is the region which presents the last frontier of our seeking to manage intelligently all that we have been given and all that we have created for ourselves. We have reasons to think that during Delta-type functioning we return so completely to the Source from which we came that we rarely remember, nor are we even aware of what transpired. We seem not to remember, that is, until we demonstrate prudential judgement in managing Beta, Alpha, and Theta dimensions much more successfully. You see, the whole process is developmental. As children mature they are capable of accomplishing much more, physically, mentally, and spiritually. And as they demonstrate that maturity, caretakers begin to entrust more to them. So it is with our overall development.

Individuals in our planet's history seem to have attained such peak fulfillment that they managed all levels. Their lives and teachings remain in writings and traditions to spur us on and guide us to such fulfillment ourselves. As we desire and believe so we, too, will achieve what they have before us, and more! We are called to nothing less. It only takes time for our fulfillment to manifest on the earth plane of existence. More and more individuals are now uplifting themselves as this planet moves into its second phase of human evolution. As the individual units of the human race uplift themselves, then all of humanity will be swept into the vortex spiralling toward fulfillment. Whether you call the New Age an Omega Point, the Aquarian Age, the Age of Cosmic Consciousness, or the Age of Love, Light, and Life, it still is the cultural uplift that each person has as rightful heritage. And our claiming our heritage will swing this whole planet toward fulfillment. For we are here to uplift, not tear down, and we will claim dominion over nature only when we establish our own control of ourselves. And that is what the Silva Method is all about.

Blending Level 1 as they do with their levels of functioning, the Mind Control graduates eventually will have so balanced all the proper levels and frequencies that they will have awakened control even of Delta. At that moment they will have mastered earth life and become the Masters they are called to be. They then have attained what might be called <u>Supra-Consciousness</u>. Such consciousness is oftentimes referred to as illumination and enlightenment, but in such a way that it is a permanent state, perfectly self-controlled. In other words, the Mind Control graduates will then have attained what is called <u>Christ</u> <u>Awareness</u>. And the experience is open to all alike — Christian, Jew, Moslem, Hindu, Atheist — after all, we are from the same Ultimate Source and we all live within the same system of law. We all call only One our Father. And the Father is within each of us.

What is so unique in the Silva Method is that Jose Silva has brought us a workable system that we can share with others. All peoples can learn to use it. It can be shared. You can learn it. And it is valid and reliable: it works! You can learn through the Silva Method to alter your levels of consciousness, bring about changes in brain chemistry that alter your brain frequencies, and use these altered levels of self-controlled awareness to solve problems, at an objective, five-senses level, or at a subjective, inner-senses level. You simply turn on (naturally, no need for drugs or electronic stimulation) and tune in. You search out the information wherever it is—simply by sensing at an outer or an inner dimension, much as a submarine searches through periscope or sonar equipment.

As you gain expertise at using the beautiful equipment your creators have given you to work with, you eventually learn to control with such intelligent management of energy that you attain more and more peak experiences of Christ Awareness until you eventually become a prominent citizen of the realm which is the second phase of human evolution on this planet. And you will do it all for yourself through the Silva Method.

After all, isn't doing it yourself the only way?

Epilogue: Concepts by Jose Silva

When the law of relativity is applied to mind and its concepts of values, concepts of values change in direct proportion to the acquisition of greater knowledge. What was our concept yesterday? What is it today? What will it be tomorrow? Our present concept of the Human Mind due to the acquisition of additional knowledge (accumulation of understandable information) is, "That the Human Mind is a sensing faculty of Human Intelligence," such as sight is the sensing faculty of the eye and hearing is of the ear. These faculties of the eyes and ears are the true sensing means of the brain. Present knowledge indicates that the sensing faculty of human intelligence is a "Master Sense" that senses information stored on brain cells, information stored by other senses. The Master Sense functions as a transmitter or receiver; it's a faculty that is adjustable by resonant, directed desires. It can impress (influence) and/or detect (sense) information on cell life, plant, animal or human, in the environment or at a distance.

It is to human intelligence what the periscope is to the submarine. Human intelligence can, through a desire, tune its Master Sense to any portion of the brain and can become aware of information stored there. The brain is like a filing cabinet; information has been stored in it since man first set foot on this planet and was functioning at a primitive level of animal life. This information has been passed on from father and mother to son and daughter in many ways, including the genetic means of transmission.

Knowing that our brain is serving as a filing cabinet, we should study our brain. One of the ways that scientists study the brain is electronically, by measuring its electrical output pulsations. When we are awake, the electrical pulsations of the brain are the highest, over 14 pulsations per second. When we are deep asleep, in deep slumber, the pulsations are slowest around .5 to 3.5 pulsations per second. Then there are the pulsations that take place between those extremes. These pulsations (rhythmic frequency of neurons firing) have been named by brain wave researchers, the lowest being "Delta," the highest, "Beta," and the frequencies in between, "Theta" and "Alpha." The Alpha frequency is lower and just below and next to the Beta. The part of the brain (file) whose predominant electrical output is Beta, has attached to it the so-called 5 senses (physical-objective) "Touch, Taste, Smell, Hearing and Seeing." The Beta file is then considered to be divided into many subdivisions. Apparently all information that our physical senses have contacted is filed in some sub-compartment within the Beta file.

Information is filed in the Beta files by the physical senses when a sense is stimulated by some pulsating energy; that energy pulsating at a certain rate is fed into the Beta part of the brain and mixes with the brain energy that is pulsating at a Beta frequency. We then need to consider the combined effect of the energy of two different frequencies: the Beta frequency and the frequency of the stimulus. The heterodyned (mixed) effect is the Beta frequency altered (modulated) at the rate of the stimulus frequency. Information impressed with strong stimulation at the time the Mind is sensing in a self-controlled way and the brain is receiving can be easily recalled. To recall (remember) simply tune the Master Sense (the Mind) to the stimulation frequency and the brain will fire in the same pattern as when the impression was made.

The receptive frequency of the brain when receiving outside objective stimulation is very important. When this frequency is non-synchronized and weak, impressions from outside are less effective. When this frequency is synchronized and strong, the impressions are very effective and recall is enhanced. Once information has been strongly impressed through physical senses (Beta senses) in the Beta part of the brain (in Beta neurons) we can recall this information (re-trigger the firing of neurons chain-like in their established neural pathways) by tuning our vibrating Master Sense (the Mind) to resonate to the particular frequency of the objective stimulation that impressed the original information. A desire to remember projects our Master Sense (the Mind) back to tune to a past impression and fires the Beta neurons in a chain-like manner, firing in the same way they had fired when originally triggered by the external stimulation. This process is what we know as recall.

Humans can learn to project their Master Sense (the Mind) to the Alpha-producing part of their brain and function from that perspective with awareness. The Alpha-producing part of brain is a dimension within itself, apparently a dimension which had been neglected in human evolution. The Alpha dimension has a complete set of sensing faculties like the Beta. At Beta the objective stimuli find their way into the Beta neurons and the Master Sense senses this information subjectively. At Alpha subjective stimuli find their way into

Alpha neurons and the Master Sense being subjective senses this information directly. A copy of all information reaching Beta neurons is transferred and impressed at the Alpha dimension on the Alpha-producing part of the brain, in Alpha neurons. The Beta senses that detect and impress information on the Beta part of brain are called objective senses. The Alpha senses that detect and impress information on the Alpha part of the brain are called subjective senses. Using the objective senses to communicate and learn, will be considered as objective communication and objective education. Using the subjective for the same purpose will be subjective communication and subjective education. Since we were not using the Alpha dimension with awareness, we now need to educate ourselves to function at this dimension, to guide, direct and orient our Psyche (Mind). This is the new science of Psychorientology (Psyche-Orientation), the study of orienting Mind in the subjective world of the Mind dimension. This is known as Subjective Education and is what Mind Control is all about. One of the most important discoveries resulting from the research in Psychorientology is subjective communication, the ability of one Mind (the Master Sense) to detect information impressed on another brain at a distance. This type of detection of information from a brain at a distance is taking place at the Alpha dimension, and this is our concept of Subjective Communication. Once people learn to enter the Alpha dimension they then need to learn to function proficiently at Alpha as they have learned to do at Beta.

People can project Mind (the Master Sense) to the Beta region of Brain with the intention of getting information that was previously impressed. They must have some idea of what they are looking for; if so, they cause Mind to function as a transmitter, transmitting a frequency that is identical to the frequency of one of the factors of the impressed information. When the frequency of Mind becomes resonant to that factor, this triggers the firing of that particular chain of neurons causing a playback of that chain of impressions. We then have recall by what is usually known as association. It is easier for Mind to lock on to stronger impressions than to weaker ones. Information is strongly impressed on brain cells when the information is relative to survival; this information can be tuned to with little effort. Now that we know how to project Mind to the Alpha region of the brain, we find that at this dimension we also have the means to detect information impressed on the Alpha region of the brain, in Alpha neurons. We find that when the Beta senses (Physical senses) detect and impress information on the Beta region of the brain in Beta neurons, this information is at the same time being automatically impressed on the Alpha region of the brain in Alpha neurons. It appears that the Physical senses are an extension of the Psychic (subjective) Alpha senses, so that everything impressed in Beta neurons is also impressed in Alpha neurons. The physical stimuli are impressed in Beta neurons by Beta senses only when a person's Master Sense, Mind, is aware of such impressions. When the person is not aware, the information bypasses the Beta neurons and is subliminally impressed in Alpha neurons. The Mind when projected to function from the Beta perspective cannot become aware of the bypassed information; it can only do so from the Alpha perspective. The person when functioning from the Alpha perspective can direct psychic senses to detect information, impress it, in Alpha neurons and recall it in the future; can sense information previously impressed or presently being impressed in Alpha neurons; can detect the information that bypassed the Beta neurons; can from this perspective also sense the information previously impressed or presently being impressed on Beta neurons.

Learning to function from the Alpha perspective is of tremendous value when we consider what has been covered so far; but this is not all. The greatest discovery of all is that Mind (Master Sense) can be projected to function from the Alpha perspective and can be oriented to develop controls by a person establishing points of reference within the Alpha dimension. The Mind can learn to sense information impressed not only in its own Alpha neurons but can sense information impressed in the Alpha neurons of other brains, regardless of distance. It staggers the imagination to consider that all information which is impressed on Beta and Alpha neurons, regardless of a person's awareness of Beta and/or Alpha senses making such impressions, is now available to the human being.

We human beings with our Intelligence can learn to enter the Alpha dimension; through Psychorientology we can learn to develop controls in establishing points of reference for proficient functioning within the subjective dimension. With the development of such proficiency, the human being can function at the Alpha dimension whenever there is a need; we can project Controlled Mind, making use of previously established points of reference, to sense information impressed in neurons of any brain that is on this planet, or a brain that is on any planet within our solar system, any solar system within our galaxy or on any galaxy within our universe. Persons who develop as much proficiency in functioning at Alpha as they have developed at Beta can develop the means to function automatically within both dimensions depending on survival needs. Persons who through training themselves develop automatic responses at both Beta and Alpha dimensions become healthier, more productive and better problem solving agents on this planet.

To start learning to use the Alpha dimension with controlled awareness is like being born again. It is starting from the beginning to establish original points of reference as we did when we were born and established the first points of reference at the Beta dimension. Humanity is developing to full proficiency the use of Beta senses to detect, program and store information (knowledge) in the Beta region of brain. Humanity has also developed the ability to project Mind (the Master Sense) to sense the stored information (knowledge) and put it to good use to solve problems. When a problem is solved, we become aware that we have used knowledge wisely; the accumulation of experiences of wisely solved problems develop into wisdom. Humanity's present concept of values is questionable to the extent that we are functioning from a very limited perspective using only one set of senses within one dimension, the Beta. The Law of Relativity is then applied to our use of Mind projected to a perspective within the Beta dimension and everything that we have done is relative to Mind limited in its function by such perspective. Humanity's wrong concepts of values reflect ignorance of not knowing we could learn to use another dimension and another set of senses. Humanity using two dimensions and two sets of senses can project Mind to function from a superior perspective; from that superior perspective we can use a larger store of knowledge, develop greater wisdom, and conceive a more realistic and truer sense of values.

Since the mind of humanity participates in everything, locating a superior mental perspective from which to function will help humanity to encompass through mental projection a greater spectrum that includes not only the planet in which we live; but also our solar system, our galaxy, and our universe, along with the possibility of including the totality of the Microcosmos and Macrocosmos. Psychorientology (Psyche Orientation) is the new science that will help humanity to develop Mind Control and use it to locate Superior Mental Perspective. Humanity will then become superior human beings; at that time we will be equipped to take the first step into the second phase of human evolution on this planet. People can start right now to develop Mind Control and through Psychorientology we can achieve our goal of finding a superior mental perspective. The first step is for us to learn to enter the Alpha dimension with awareness and to establish points of reference. We chart every step of the way so that these points of reference may again be found in the future whenever we have need of them. We thereby establish self-controlled awareness. As people learn to function at more Alpha levels with self-controlled awareness (states of consciousness), we can start practicing the use of these levels for our benefit. In Education, for example, we can learn to impress and recall information more effectively; we then can achieve higher grades (a higher I.Q. factor becomes a possibility). In Health, we can learn to relax at will any time mentally and/or physically; we can learn to enter sleep naturally without the use of drugs; we can learn to correct many undesirable habits effectively; we can learn to prevent psychosomatic disorders; through all of this we can maintain healthier bodies and minds. In Problem Solving, we can learn to communicate subjectively to obtain information from whoever has it, even at a distance, by the use of our developed psychic senses; we can also learn to use this information for problem solving, thus help ourselves become more successful and better problem-solving agents on this planet. In Religion, while acquiring proficiency to function at Alpha levels, deep within, we can become resonant with the spiritual dimension, the dimension for prayer. If we are to communicate with our creator and we have not succeeded at the world of the body dimension, it is because the body of man/woman is the son/daughter of the creator of the body of man/woman: "Man/woman is the son/daughter of man/woman." We will then succeed at the world of the mind dimension, the spiritual dimension, because there is no other alternative but that the mind of man/woman is the son/daughter of the creator of mind: "Mind is the son/daughter of God." Since deep Alpha is a spiritual dimension, it is by this dimension that we can increase our I.Q., have better health, acquire greater problem-solving potential for success and communicate with our creator, our God; all is possible within this inner dimension. We need to find and learn to use this inner kingdom, then locate our Superior Mental Perspective from which we are able to form our new and better concepts of values. This dimension is a real Heavenly Kingdom that is within us and that we can use when we need to solve problems because in functioning from this Superior Mental Perspective, "There is nothing concealed that will not be disclosed and nothing hidden that will not be made known" (Luke 12:2-3).

In the future we need to direct our emphasis to the area of meditation because of its tremendous benefits. A superior mental perspective from which to operate can be reached through mental exercises, such as those practiced in hypnosis, Yoga, Zen, Transcendental or Silva Mind Control meditation. Even biofeedback training in alpha sensing can help a person find a superior mental perspective, but for operating with awareness it must be accompanied by verbal instruction so as to use that dimension of thinking for specific applications. Whether or not a particular method of meditation requires the cutting out of all internal and external incoming stimuli, or becoming hypersensitive to internal and external stimuli, external verbal instruction is necessary for learning to function with awareness from a newly found mental perspective until we develop our own internal sense of guidance. Meditation and biofeedback help us to find the center, relaxed-thinking mental level of our brain frequency's spectrum. This is a very valuable state for health, because from this centered, mentally neutral level, there is no disturbing mental influence on the autonomic nervous system. This kind of disturbing influence is nearly always erroneous, causing the sympathetic and parasympathetic nervous systems to get out of synchronization, thereby not producing what the body needs for self-repair, and causing psychosomatic health problems. Any system of meditation, and now also biofeedback training, can help us enter into the alpha-theta brain wave range. But so doing is only the first step; it is like like entering the classroom for learning. What you learn to do once you are there is what counts. The advantage of Silva Mind Control is that not only does it help you to enter the classroom (the Alpha-Theta brain dimension) but also helps you to learn how to function with awareness within the dimension for specific purposes. It is like learning to use what was formerly known as the subconscious levels of mind but consciously. Some scientists are beginning to agree that this is possible and call it "learning to control altered states of consciousness;" others call it "thought control", "voluntary control of internal states", "psychosomatic self-regulation", "self-control of inner states of awareness", and by many other terms; but our method we chose to name Silva Mind Control.

Some so-called experts and even some not-too-versed scientists have said that the Silva Mind Control Method is nothing but hypnosis. The Alpha-Theta classroom (dimension) has many doors through which you can enter. Some are named: Magnetism, Mesmerism, Hypnotism, Yoga, Zen, Transcendental Meditation, The Art of Concentration, Prayer, fainting, shock and sleep. Yoga is not Zen; neither is Zen Hypnosis; neither is Hypnosis Silva Mind Control. Each seeks its own goals by using certain terms as tools for programming. The difference is found in the end results achieved with any method. For instance, in Hypnosis, using the terminology as used in Hypnosis and programming with it as is done in hypnotic programming, the programmed subject would respond in the following manner: the deeper the subject goes, the more he forgets; the less controls he has and he can only answer questions; he does not ask questions. He can also be lead to release control of his faculty of visualization (be made to hallucinate). With the Silva Mind Control Method, using the terminology as used in Silva Mind Control and programming with it as is done in Silva Mind Control programming, the programmed student would respond in this manner: the deeper the students go, the more they remember, the more controls they have; not only can they answer questions but they can also ask questions; and they can maintain control of their faculties of visualization and imagination (cannot be made to hallucinate). The ultimate results of programming with Silva Mind Control as compared with programming with hypnosis are completely different. So Hypnosis is not Silva Mind Control nor Yoga and Silva Mind Control is not Hypnosis nor Yoga, because each has and uses its own different terminology and uses it to program in its own different way, seeking to achieve its own different goals. The goal of Silva Mind Control is to help every human being find the Alpha-Theta dimension and learn to use it with awareness for problem solving. It is at this dimension that human beings can detect information by means other than by using their known, so-called five senses. This detection of information Silva Mind Control calls Subjective Communication and it can be used for Subjective Education, helping us to develop into superior human beings because we can then make use of two dimensions and two sets of senses instead of one.

The questions about physical (drugs, electrical) control of mind (thought control) and mental brain wave control (in and out of Alpha-Theta) continue and answers continue to be unsettled and confusing among scientists.

What is control for one scientist is not control for another; it seems that what one scientist discovers twenty scientists want to undiscover instead of to help discover more. If we could only establish a law for scientists that before any scientist tries to tear apart anyone's discovery, that the scientist be prepared to replace it with something better, we would really get ahead. In our case some scientists have said that we should not say that with Silva Mind Control we can control the brain-waves, unless we are attached to an EEG or to Alpha-Theta biofeedback sensors. If the control they mean is getting in and out of the Alpha-Theta dimension (in = Alpha-Theta brain wave output; out = Beta brain wave output), then it can be stated that it has been proven that students of Silva Mind Control can learn to get in and out at will. Concerning the use of Alpha-Theta sensors for testing let us state that it gets a little tiresome, especially when you have tested a few thousand and get the same results, more so when you have found a different way of testing that is simpler, less expensive and just as accurate for our purpose.

Silva Mind Control, the Active Dynamic Meditation System is down to earth, scientific, fast, effective, simple, economical and just right for the world. Many imitators of our work are starting to appear; many more will continue to appear. Accept no imitation. Go for the original, the creators of the first method in history that offers you controlled Effective Sensory Projection (E.S.P.), Subjective Communication, and Subjective Education through the Silva Method as presented by Silva Mind Control International, Inc., Laredo, Texas, U.S.A., the Creators of MIND CONTROL®.

In subsequent books we will consider and discuss education, religion, the healing arts and problem solving in general from a superior mental perspective achieved through Psychorientology.

## A select bibliography

Altered states of consciousness. (Ed. Charles T. Tart) New York: John Wiley and Sons, Inc., 1969.

Andersen, U. S. The greatest power in the universe. Los Angeles, California: Atlantis University, 1971.

Backster, C. "Evidence of a primary perception in plant life." International Journal of Parapsychology, 1968, 10, 329-348.

Barber, Theodore X. LSD, marihuana, yoga, and hypnosis. Chicago: Aldine Publishing Company, 1970.

Biofeedback and self control 1970, 1971, 1972, 1973, 1974. (Eds. Theodore X. Barber, L.V. Di Cara, J. Kamiya, N. E. Miller, D. Shapiro, J. Stoyva.) Chicago: Aldine-Atherton, 1971.

Brown, Barbara. New Mind, New Body. New York: Harper and Row, 1974.

Cantor, Alfred J. Ridding yourself of psychosomatic health-wreckers. West Nyack, New York: Parker Publishing Co., Inc., 1965.

Dean, D., Mihalasky J., Ostrander, S., & Schroeder, L. Executive ESP. Englewood Cliffs, N. J.: Prentice Hall, Inc., 1974.

Delgado, Jose M. R. Physical control of the mind. New York: Harper and Row, 1969.

Fast, Julius. Body language. New York: Pocket Books, 1971.

Guzman, Emilio. Mind Control - New Dimension of Human Thought. Mexico City, 1972. Also available in a Spanish version.

Hutschnecker, Arnold A. The Will To Live. New York: Cornerstone Library, 1966.

Huxley, Aldous. Brave new world. New York and Evanston: Harper and Row, 1946.

Karagulla, Shafica. Breakthrough to creativity. Los Angeles: DeVorss and Co., Inc., 1967.

Kooi, Kenneth A. Fundamentals of electroencephalography. New York: Harper and Row, 1971.

Kruger, Helen. Other Healers, Other Cures. Indianapolis/ N. Y.: The Bobbs-Merrill Co., Inc., 1974.

Learning approaches to therapeutic behavior change. (Ed. Donald J. Lewis) Chicago: Aldine Publishing Co., 1970.

Lecomte du Nouy, Pierre. Human destiny. New York: David McKay Co., Inc., 1947.

London, Perry. Behavior control. New York: Harper and Row, 1969.

Luce, Gay Gaer, and Segal, Julius. Sleep. New York: Coward-McCann, Inc., 1966.

Maltz, Maxwell. Psycho-cybernetics. Hollywood, California: Wilshire Book Co., 1960.

Moss, Thelma. The Probability of the Impossible. Los Angeles: J. P. Tarcher, Inc., 1974.

Orwell, George. 1984. New York: Harcourt, Brace, and World, 1949.

Ostrander, Sheila and Schroeder, Lynn. Psychic discoveries behind the iron curtain. Englewood Cliffs, New Jersey: Prentice Hall, Inc., 1970

Oyle, Irving. The Healing Mind. Millbrae, Calif: Celestial Arts, 1975.

Research Studies of Silva Mind Control, A Compendium. Laredo, Tex.: Institute of Psychorientology, Inc., 1975.

Rhine, Louisa E. Mind over matter. New York: The Macmillan Company, 1970.

Simeons, A. T. W. Man's presumptuous brain. New York: E. P. Dutton, Inc., 1960.

Spalding, Baird T. Life and teachings of the masters of the far east. Los Angeles: DeVorss and Co., 1964. (5 volumes).

Sugrue, Thomas. There is a river. New York: Dell Publishing Co., Inc., 1945.

Teilhard de Chardin, Pierre. The phenomenon of man. London: Wm. Collins and Sons, 1959.

The Holy Bible (Revised Standard Version). New York: Thomas Nelson and Sons, 1946 and 1952.

The Urantia Book. Chicago: Urantia Foundation, 1955.

Toben, Bob. Space-Time and Beyond. New York: E. P. Dutton & Co., Inc., 1975.

Ullman, Montague, and Krippner, Stanley. Dream studies and telepathy: An experimental approach. New York: Parapsychology Foundation, Inc., 1970.

Walter, W. Grey. The living brain. New York: W. W. Norton and Co., Inc., 1963.

Yogananada, Paramahansa. Autobiography of a yogi. Los Angeles: Self-Realization Fellowship, 1959.

# SCALE OF BRAIN EVOLUTION

| Level | Brain Wave | State |
|---|---|---|
| OUTER CONSCIOUS LEVELS | BETA | 21 |
| INNER CONSCIOUS LEVELS | ALPHA | 14 |
| | BASIC PLANE THETA | 7 |
| UNCONSCIOUS | DELTA | 4 |

SLEEP / THOUGHT

**PHYSICAL WORLD** — SIGHT, SOUND, SMELL, TOUCH, TASTE — TIME SPACE

**SPIRITUAL WORLD** — NO TIME SPACE — E S P

**?**

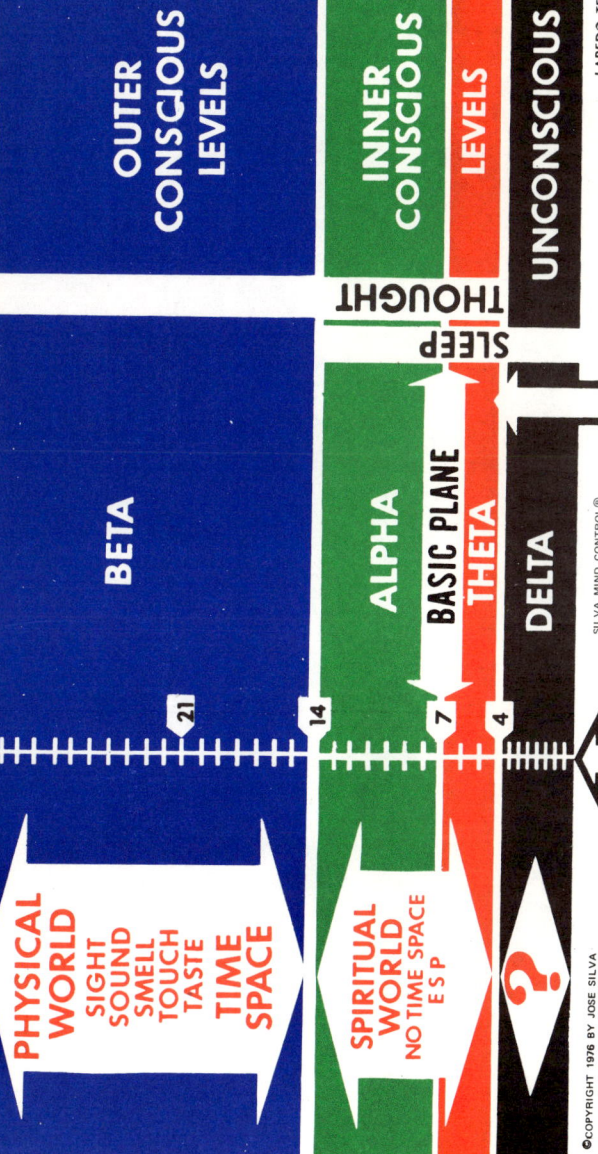

BRAIN RHYTHM (CYCLES PER SEC.)

THESE LEVELS FOR PAINLESS SURGERY, DENTISTRY, CHILDBIRTH, ETC.

SILVA MIND CONTROL®
© COPYRIGHT 1976 BY JOSE SILVA
LAREDO, TEXAS